Economics Revision Guide

Other books in this series

Cost Accounting Revision Guide   Colin Drury
Quantitative Methods Revision Guide   Paul Goodwin

Economics Revision Guide

Rob Dixon and Keith West

Heinemann Professional Publishing

Heinemann Professional Publishing Ltd
Halley Court, Jordan Hill, Oxford OX2 8EJ

OXFORD   LONDON   MELBOURNE   AUCKLAND

First published 1988

© Rob Dixon and Keith West 1988

British Library Cataloguing in Publication Data
Dixon, R. (Rob)
  Economics revision guide.
  1. Economics
  I. title   II. West, Keith
  330

ISBN 0 434 92364 8

Typeset by Keyset Composition, Colchester, Essex
Printed and bound by Richard Clay Ltd, Chichester

Contents

Preface

This book has been commissioned by the CIMA and Heinemann as a revision guide. It is aimed principally at CIMA Level 1 economics students but it is most useful for other professional and A level economics students too. The relevant courses are outlined on page 3.

A condensed form has been used to enable easy and quick reference. The bulk of the book is contained in Part Two's Revision Notes. Each chapter is subdivided into four sections which reveal the relationship with other topics, underlying concepts, points of perspective and essential knowledge.

These are accompanied by most valuable informal notes which stress important general points, give examples and indicate interrelationships with other ideas. The latter feature is particularly useful in the later sections where the subject 'comes together'. The informal notes are a vital aid in structuring an answer to an examination question.

Past exam questions and a test paper are given to illustrate the demands of the relevant exams. In addition, summary answers have been written to show the depth of knowledge and conceptual understanding required.

We would like to thank Mark Wright, the Publisher at the CIMA and Kathryn Grant and Deena Cook, our editors at Heinemann for their confidence in us and their interested support and guidance.

However, we are particularly indebted to our wives and typists for their help, encouragement and efficiency.

Rob Dixon, Keith West
June 1988

Part One
How to Use this Book

1 The text in Part Two will give you the key information on each topic. The chart on page 3 shows how the topics relate to the various syllabuses.

Pay special attention to the informal notes which are set next to the main text. These highlight important concepts and show links with other ideas in other topics.

2 In Part Three there are worked examples of past examination questions. It is advisable to attempt these without referring to the text in each chapter. If your answers disagree significantly with those given, then re-read the appropriate part of the chapter.

3 Part Four outlines some problems and pitfalls. It gives many hints on exam technique and guidance on proper preparation for the exams.

4 Towards the end of your revision you should take the Test Paper in Part Five. This will give you practice in answering questions under examination conditions.

This revision guide covers comprehensively the following syllabuses:

- Chartered Institute of Management Accountants – Stage 1 Economics
- Chartered Institute of Bankers (CIOB) – Foundation Course
- Institute of Chartered Accountants (ICA) – Foundation Course
- Chartered Association of Certified Accountants – 1.3 Economics
- London Chamber of Commerce and Industry – Economics Interim (2017)
- London Chamber of Commerce and Industry – Economics Higher (3017)
- Royal Society of Arts – Stage III Advanced Economics (QP 322)
- Institute of Chartered Secretaries and Administrators – Part 1 Economics

- Institute of Marketing – Certificate
- A Level (all Boards) Economics

As can be seen from the following analysis it also makes a useful contribution to the parts of some more specialist courses:

- Chartered Institute of Bankers – Final – Economics and Banks' Role in Economy
- Chartered Institute of Bankers – Final – Monetary Economics
- Chartered Association of Certified Accountants – 2.5c Management Economics

Syllabus analysis

	Chapter 1 Economics and society	Chapter 2 Economic structures	Chapter 3 Supply and demand	Chapter 4 Labour	Chapter 5 Money and banking	Chapter 6 Macroeconomics	Chapter 7 Government and the economy	Chapter 8 International trade
CIMA – Stage 1 Economics	*	*	*	*	*	*	*	*
CIOB – Foundation	*	*	*	*	*	*	*	*
ICA – Foundation	*	*	*	*	*	*	*	*
CACA – 1.3 Economics	*	*	*	*	*	*	*	*
LCCI – Economics Interim	*	*	*	*	*	*	*	*
LCCI – Economics Higher	*	*	*	*	*	*	*	*
RSA – Stage III Advanced	*	*	*	*	*	*	*	*
ICSA – Part 1 Economics	*	*	*	*	*	*	*	*
IM	*	*	*	*	*	*	*	*
A Level Economics	*	*	*	*	*	*	*	*
CIOB – Final – Economics and Banks' Role in Economy	*		*		*			*
CIOB – Final – Monetary Economics					*			*
CACA – 2.5c Management Economics		*	*					*

Part Two
Revision Notes

1
Economics and society

1.1 Topic relationship

This chapter provides an outline of the fundamental concepts, terms, methods and systems of which economics consists. It seeks to show how these fundamentals relate to other disciplines, and, indeed, the interdisciplinary nature of economics. It also seeks to show the part of economics in society, or more particularly, the economic nature of society.

Economics is the study of the *creation* and *distribution of wealth*. One of the primary concerns of economics is to increase the wealth of society. Yet, in addition to wealth we must also consider *welfare*. The concept of welfare is concerned with the whole state of well-being. Thus it is not only concerned with more economic goods but also with public health, hours of work, law and order etc. Central to the study of wealth is the *concept of price*.

Economics is influenced by many other disciplines. It is influenced by politics and also by sociology, history, psychology and mathematics.

Economics, to be a practical *social science*, must fulfil two functions:

1 It must help people to understand economic events in the real world.
2 It must enable people to make predictions about economic phenomena.

The study of economic problems is difficult because of the complex nature of the world, i.e. the complicated interdependencies between and within societies and the different and changing behaviour of individuals themselves.

By wealth we understand all the real physical assets which make up our standard of living.

To increase the stock of economic goods.

It is possible to increase wealth without increasing welfare; the wealth/welfare connotation is thus a complex aspect of the subject.

The exchange value of goods and services arising out of scarcity of resources and competing demands for those resources.

1.2 Underlying concepts

Four basic concepts underlie economic thinking: scarcity and choice; opportunity cost; interdependence, and efficiency.

1.2.1 Scarcity and choice

Resources are *scarce* and therefore the unlimited *wants* of *consumers* cannot be fulfilled. Consequently *choices* must be made as to which wants will be fulfilled and which will be *forgone*.

1.2.2   *Opportunity cost*

The forgone alternative arising out of a choice is known as the *opportunity cost*. This usually has a *monetary value* but if the choice involves alternatives with *zero price* then it will have no monetary value.

1.2.3   *Interdependence*

As people *specialize* in jobs, they are not in themselves self-sufficient and become *dependent* on others in society.

1.2.4   *Efficiency*

Economics is concerned with the *efficient* use of *scarce resources*.

1.3   Points of perspective

This chapter focuses on the fundamentals of economics and the economic workings of society, highlighting the fact that economics is not a discipline operating in a vacuum, but that it influences and is influenced by numerous 'other' factors. Perhaps the major factor which influences economics and is in turn influenced by economics is government/political. The section on economic systems is relative to what is called '*political economy*'.

The area of political economy and the economic nature of society has produced a wealth of economic/political theories and ideologies. These need to be taken into consideration if you are to study and understand the interaction and relationship between economics and the human environment. Those who have had something to say about economics and the human race have had a profound influence on human economic and political systems and thinking. What is quite clear from all of these theorists despite their profoundly different approaches and conclusions is that man is an economic animal and that economics cannot be divorced from man and his whole environment.

They include Adam Smith (The Wealth of Nations), John Stuart Mill (Principles of Political Economy), Karl Marx (Das Kapital), and in more recent years John Maynard Keynes and Milton Friedman.

1.4   Essential knowledge

1.4.1   *Economic terms*

Students of economics soon discover that although economists use everyday words they very often use them in a different context to mean quite different things.

(a)   *Capital*:   This is one of the most elusive of all the terms used by economists, since it is employed in a number of different senses. To the layman, 'capital' may mean something like '*accumulated wealth*', to the businessman, 'capital' may mean the *fund* or *stock* with which he enters into business. The economist, too, uses 'capital' in both these senses, but he also uses it in an additional sense as meaning all the *man-made aids* used to further production such as *machinery*, *plant*, *equipment* and *factory buildings*, which are not *consumed* for their own sake but which are used up in the process of making other goods. Thus when economists write about the accumulation of capital, what is primarily meant is the process of adding to the nation's stock of man-made aids to further production. They may also be referring to the *monetary reflection* of this process.

The accumulation of the money funds required to purchase the additional capital goods.

(b) *Commodity*: In economics this is the word used to describe an *article* or good which is produced with the aim of *selling* or *exchanging* it for something else.

(c) *Consumption*: Economics uses the term to mean the act of using something or using it up.

(d) *Cost*: To the layman, the 'cost' of an article usually means what he has to pay for it i.e. its *money price*. In economics the 'cost' of an article usually means what has to be given up or sacrificed in order to produce it.

(e) *Demand*: This is the amount of a commodity which consumers are prepared to buy. It always refers to the amount bought over some specific *period* of time, at some specific *price*.

(f) *Distribution*: This may be used in the sense of getting goods to factories or consumers but it is most often used to mean the process whereby the goods and services produced in a country are shared out among different individuals and groups of people.

(g) *National income*: This is the *flow* of newly produced goods and services produced by the residents of a nation over a given period of time.

(h) *Wealth*: The 'sum total of saleable assets with a monetary value'.

(i) *Firm and industry*: A firm is a business whereas an industry is a collection of firms making similar products.

(j) *Utility*: The '*satisfaction derived* from the *consumption* of a good or service'.

(k) *Production and productivity*: Production refers to the *total output* of a firm whereas productivity refers to output per person.

1.4.2 *Economic methods*

The task of economic theory is to simplify the real world so that economic phenomena can be examined and understood.

The scientific method as applied in economics requires the building of economic theories which necessitates:

(a) Selection of the economic *variables* to be studied.

(b) Identification of *assumptions* i.e. specification of the relationships between economic variables.

(c) Formulation of *hypotheses* about economic behaviour.

(d) Construction of theories (*models*).

(e) Testing of theories, i.e. comparing what the theory predicts will happen with what actually does happen in the world.

(f)   The testing of theories requires factual knowledge, therefore statistical data is essential.

In developing hypotheses economists make two basic simplifying assumptions. First, that human behaviour is *rational*; the second assumption they work on is that of *ceteris paribus*.

All other things being equal or remaining constant.

In developing theories economists can take one of two approaches. They can follow a course of *inductive reasoning* in which they rely on an orderly collection of data, using it as a basis for generalization about economic behaviour. Alternatively economists can adopt the approach of *deductive reasoning* in which they proceed by logical reasoning from a set of basic observations and operating assumptions, following systematically the implications of logical reference arising from this premise, to a set of conclusions about the probable shape of other unobserved phenomena.

Increasingly economic analysts are employing both methods, beginning with deductive reasoning and ending by using the inductive approach as a check on the results obtained from the first method. Both approaches to economic theory suffer from the weakness of changing circumstances.

The point or purpose of developing an economic theory is that it is designed to look at a problem by examining the works of a unit, its reactions to outside factors and its resultant behaviour. It *simplifies* reality, although it must maintain credence.

1.4.3   The economic problem

Allocation of scarce resources

The economic *problem* arises because people lack *resources* to fulfil their many desires. Most resources have to be bought and thus have a price. The owners of resources can command higher *prices* for their resources if they are scarce. Due to *scarcity* of resources, *choices* have to be made between *competing* ends. The choice of where resources will be *allocated* involves making an *opportunity cost judgement*. This allocation of resources has a twofold objective as follows:

(a)   To facilitate the most *efficient* use of resources.
(b)   To increase the well-being of society i.e. improve *standards of living*.

A concern to reduce pollution, violence, crime, pornography etc.

Within the objective of improving living standards we can identify a *welfare approach* to economics which places emphasis on the *quality of life* as an important aspect of the standard of living.

1.4.4   Production decisions

What to produce, where to produce, how to produce, how to distribute?

The allocation of resources involves making *production decisions*. These production decisions which are made in order to resolve the economic problem are continually assessed using the criteria of rationality, efficiency and fairness.

The economic resources which are used in tackling the economic problem can be identified in the following categories:

(a)   *Natural resources* – land, gases, vegetation.
(b)   *Human resources* – people.
(c)   *Man-made resources* – capital goods.

These can be reclassified into four categories:

(a) *Land*:   This is largely limited in supply. Technological advances such as reclamation only marginally expand the land supply.
(b) *Labour*:   This is a human resource and it is determined by population size. General influences on labour supply include age and sex distribution, laws, immigration policy, social customs etc.
(c) *Enterprise*:   A human resource concerned with decision making.
(d) *Capital*:   A man-made resource aiding production.

1.4.5   Types of production

There are three types of production as follows:

(a) *Primary production*:   This is the *extraction* of raw materials from the earth's surface.

Agriculture, oil drilling.

(b) *Secondary production*:   This area of production is concerned with the *conversion* of raw materials into finished products.
(c) *Tertiary production*:   This is the *provision* of *services* for society. These services may be either *commercial* or *social*. Commercial services are at a price which gives *profit* to the provider e.g. hotel accommodation.

Social services are provided at a zero price or at a nominal charge which does not cover the production cost.

1.4.6   Economic systems

Economic systems can be classified according to the *allocative mechanism* employed or according to *ownership of resources*. Under the former we can identify three types of economic system:

(a) *Planned economy*:   Decisions regarding the allocation of resources are made by a *centralized body*.
(b) *Free or market economy*:   Resources are allocated through the *price mechanism*.
(c) *Mixed economy*:   Some resources are allocated in a *planned* way and others in a *market* way.

Under the classification according to ownership we can again identify three types of system:

(a) *Capitalism*:   A system in which one class of private individuals owns the *means* of *production*.
(b) *Socialism*:   Resources are owned by the society as a whole.
(c) *Mixed*:   This contains both a *public* and *private sector* with the relative size of each sector being determined by political consideration.

Joseph Schumpeter, a Harvard economist defined socialism as '. . . an institutional pattern in which the control over means of production and over production itself is vested with a central authority – or . . . (where) the economic affairs of society belong to the public and not the private sphere'.

The two forms of classification are not mutually exclusive. Generally one can equate capitalism with the *market determination* of employment, investment, resource and product allocation and a market-determined pattern of income distribution. Similarly socialist economic organization is characterized by *government ownership* of physical capital, allocation of capital and consumer goods via *central planning* and the distribution of income according to the views of central planners. However, it is possible to have resources owned communally through *collectives*, which sell on the open market, as happens in Yugoslavia where the system is called '*market socialism*'.

The planned economy

In a planned economy all production decisions are made by the government on behalf of the community. The production plans are based on the planners' perception of the people's needs. Their assessment of these needs, however, tends to be *arbitrary* and it is *political wants* rather than economic needs which tend to be satisfied. A further weakness of the planned economy lies in the distribution of goods and services to consumers. Prices are set by the *state*, often failing to reflect *demand* and *supply* conditions and instead set to induce certain responses. This creates *producer sovereignty* with consumption being determined by price. Further weaknesses lie in the lack of *incentives*, the maintenance of a large inefficient body of planners and the deterrence of risk taking due to political favouritism and an unwieldy bureaucracy.

On the plus side, a planned economy facilitates the full *utilization* of resources; it also facilitates economic *growth* as resources can be allocated away from consumption and towards *investment*. Also *economies of scale* can be obtained through the concentration of production in large units, use of specialists and the elimination of wasteful competition.

The market economy

The price mechanism allocates resources in a pure market economy, and there is *no* government interference. Prices respond to demand as do the producers and thus the consumer is sovereign in the market economy. The system is economically efficient as production reacts to price movements and the allocation of resources changes to fit more accurately the demands of the consumer.

In the market economy production is geared towards meeting the wants of those with *consumption power*; this leads to the production of *profitable luxuries*, whilst basic unprofitable services may be neglected.

Resources can be wasted in a market economy as firms may compete for the same market. If one firm emerges from that *competition* victorious then a *monopoly* could arise.

The mixed economy

All modern economies are mixed to some extent. In the free market economy there is a tendency for the market mechanism to produce undesirable or *harmful goods* and fail to produce 'necessary' goods, e.g. education for the poor. Consequently there is a need for public provision and public deterrence regarding production, which is a feature of the mixed economy.

The Yugoslavian economy is a hybrid between centralized planning and market direction. In industrial cities Yugoslavs are permitted to own and operate small scale enterprises, employing up to a maximum of five workers. In agriculture, farmers can privately own up to twenty-five acres. Also some business firms — law firms, hotels, restaurants etc. — are operated by private entrepreneurs. The bulk of economic activity, however, (80–90 per cent) is conducted by worker-managed socially-owned business firms.

This is the reduction of the average cost per unit by the spreading of fixed costs over more units.

No pure free market economy exists. Governments have become involved in economic decision making to some extent to protect the consumer and prevent economic 'bads' like pollution.

A monopoly exists where there is only one seller or supplier of a good, and thus a single firm can influence the price in the market.

1.4.7 Public provision

In the mixed economy the public sector produces what are known as *merit goods* and *public goods*.

Merit goods are those goods which are considered important for everyone. These are therefore provided by the public sector according to need at no cost to the consumer. Such goods and services are provided by the government because otherwise people might not be prepared to pay for them or buy them because of ignorance, lack of information or inadequacy of income.

Education, health care.

Public goods, such as *defence*, are also provided by the government. The market cannot be left to provide such a service because consumers could refuse to pay the price and yet still benefit from the service.

The government also provides *uneconomic* goods and services which the market sector is not prepared to supply in the quantity sought by government.

Coal and steel were once produced in loss-making industries which were subsequently nationalized.

1.4.8 Public deterrence

Some goods produced by the market may be harmful or dangerous and hence in a mixed economy the government may take steps to deter or ban their production.

These demerit goods range from drugs and child pornography to goods whose production and sale are acceptable to society but whose method of production is unacceptable because of the creation of bad externalities such as pollution.

The government can carry out public deterrence and manipulate the distribution of goods and services in a number of ways as follows:

(a) By the provision of essential goods at *zero price*.
(b) By the provision of desirable goods at *subsidized prices*.
(c) By the *taxation* of potentially harmful goods, thereby raising their market price.
(d) By imposing *fines* on the creation of *bad externalities*.

The public financing policies of government can also affect the distribution of goods.

1.4.9 Economic development

Irrespective of the type of economic system, the development made by the economies of various nations differs. We can identify three broad stages of economic development as follows:

(a) *Advanced*: Characterized by high per capita incomes, large percentage of employment in service sector, modern *infrastructure*, high standards of health, housing, education etc. For example UK, USA.
(b) *Newly industrialized*: Characterized by a growing industrial base geared to increasing exports, friction between the traditional social fabric and new development.
(c) *Less developed*: Characterized by low incomes per head, agricultural dominance, low literacy, low life expectancy, poor infrastructure, little industrial development, vulnerability to natural disaster.

Revision Questions

1   Identify and describe the major types of economic system which may be classified according to the allocative mechanism employed.
2   Outline the characteristics of the price system and the command system. Explain why most economies display characteristics of a 'mixed' economic system.

2
Economic structures

2.1 Topic relationship

This chapter examines economic *structure* in which we are concerned with the different types of business units, cost and profit theories of industrial production and industrial location. This is the heart of what is commonly known as *industrial economics* or *industrial organization*.

2.2 Underlying concepts

Business units are a fundamental part of the economic structure. They were once described by Sir Dennis Robertson the Cambridge economist as 'islands of conscious power in this ocean of unconscious cooperation, like lumps of butter coagulating in a pail of buttermilk'. Business units vary in size and according to type of ownership.

Business units are not static but are *changing* structures; the quantitative changes they undergo constitute what is known as *growth*. Growth is a fundamental concept for business units as they seek to *expand* or *integrate*.

One particular aim of growth or expansion is to attain *economies of scale*. Economies of scale may be either '*internal*' or '*external*'. Internal economies are those which are open to a single firm independently of the action of other firms, resulting from an increase in the scale of *output* of the firm. External economies are those which are shared by a number of firms or industries when the scale of *production* in any industry or group of industries increases.

The traditional theory of the firm is one of *profit maximization*; this has been criticized on a number of grounds; and alternative theories have been proposed.

A final concept which underlies the whole area of industrial organization is that of *localization*. The location of an industry in a particular region or country is determined by a number of factors: natural environment, economic, political, etc. Localization carries a number of advantages for industry but may also be the cause of serious social problems which facilitate the need for the implementation of a *regional policy* by government.

The theory of profit maximization holds that the objective of a business is to make and maximize profits — and that this will happen where total revenue exceeds total cost by the greatest amount.

Localization is the concentration of an industry in a particular area.

2.3 Points of perspective

Business units exist for the purpose of *organization* of *production*. In economics the firm is treated as a unit of *control* in which decisions are taken about what is to be produced and how it is to be produced. In conditions of *private enterprise*, most firms are privately owned and managed but some undertakings are state owned and run. There is an antithesis in the principles governing the public and the private sector – often the former involves the provision of services free of charge or the employment of workers on tasks that yield no product measurable in terms of money.

2.4   Essential knowledge

2.4.1   *Business units*

There are a number of different types of *business unit* but a basic distinction can be made according to size i.e. between *large* firms and *small* firms.

It is difficult to define 'large' firms and 'small' firms but a large firm can be said to employ over 500 employees, and a small firm less than fifty.

A number of types of firm can be placed in the large firm category as follows:

(a) *Public joint stock companies*:   A joint stock company is owned by a group of *shareholders* and pursues its business activities under the management of a *board of directors*. The *shares* of such a company are made available to the public on the *Stock Exchange*. By this means it is possible to tap the savings of a large number of people, without requiring them to take part in management of the company. The shareholders provide the *capital* of the company and assume a *limited liability* for its debts. In return they receive stocks, shares, debentures etc. entitling them to an income in the form of *dividends* on their stocks and shares or *interest* on their debentures. Depending on the terms on which they have supplied capital shareholders may have the right to elect directors.

Limited liability means that the investor is only liable to lose the money he has already invested and is not responsible for settling any debts beyond that.

(b) *Public corporations and nationalized industries*: Public corporations are public owned concerns under the control of the government but unlike *nationalized industries* they do not sell goods and services and do not gain *revenue* from their customers. In the 1978 *White Paper* on nationalized industries it was recognized that profitability alone would not be a sufficient measure of *performance* due to the *monopoly* some nationalized industries have. Instead the nationalized industries were asked to select and publish appropriate and relevant real *indicators* of performance.

Nationalized industries were created by Acts of Parliament and are publicly owned but usually are not required to make a profit.

> The indicators will vary from industry to industry . . . however, there will probably be some indicators common to most including, for example, labour, productivity and standards of service, where these are readily measurable. (Cmnd 7131, para. 78)

(c) *Cooperative retail and wholesale societies*:   These business *organizations* are part of the private sector but do not operate on the basis of profit as the primary motive. Participation in ownership is open to any purchaser for £1. Such organizations are overtly political, sponsoring MPs and maintaining close links with the Labour Party.

The types of firms which can be placed in the small firm category are as follows:

(a) *Private limited companies*:   These are companies which sell shares privately and are therefore not quoted on the Stock Exchange.
(b) *Partnerships*:   A company operating on a partnership business must have between two and twenty partners. Each partner has *unlimited liability*, unless the partnership is specifically limited in the *partner-ship deed*.
(c) *Sole proprietors*:   There are over 2.5 million self-employed people in the UK operating their own businesses.
(d) *Producer cooperatives*:   Different from cooperative societies in that these are formed and managed by groups of workers who have usually bought out their former employer. These companies tend to be profit-seeking, operating *democratically* through *committees*.

A person with unlimited liability is responsible for the debts of a firm with all his/her capital i.e. cash, property, possessions etc.

2.4.2   Nationalization

Nationalization involves the *compulsory acquisition* of property. This requires *parliamentary* approval with parliament establishing the terms of *compensation*. The various nationalization Acts invest formal powers of control with a government *minister*. The precise details of the powers given to ministers vary under the *statutes*, but they are roughly as follows: to appoint the members of the boards; to give the boards general directions in the *national interest*; and to approve *investment programmes*. Ministers have further powers which include control over financial *borrowing* of the industry subject to the approval of parliament; to approve the form of the accounts; and sometimes to approve programmes of *research* and *development*.

The various acts of nationalization imply two types of obligation for nationalized industries:
● To be *responsive* to the public interest.
● To act as *commercial* concerns.

Economic motives for nationalization
We can identify a number of economic motives for nationalization:

(a) Facilitates economies of scale.
(b) Avoids wasteful duplication.
(c) Prevents consumer exploitation.
(d) Facilitates the provision of sufficient capital for large-scale development.
(e) A desire to provide an uneconomic service.
(f) The need to control industries of strategic importance.
(g) The wish to prolong the life of a declining industry.

It must be noted, however, that decision making in nationalized industries is not always based on economic principles, as frequently there is direct *political interference*.

2.4.3   *The growth of business units*

A firm may seek to expand for two basic reasons:

- The prospect of lower *production costs* resulting from economies of scale.
- The prospect of *higher prices* resulting from a bargaining advantage or the winning of monopoly power.

There are two paths of expansion as follows:

(a)   *Internal expansion* in which the firm seeks to extend its own plant and fight for a larger share of the market.

A recent example of a merger or takeover is that of British Airways and British Caledonian.

(b)   *Integration* in which the firm seeks to *combine* with another firm either by a *merger* or by a *takeover*. In the former case there is an *amalgamation* of at least two firms into one organization; in the latter the initiative for *acquisition* must come from an offering company. Regulation of mergers and takeovers is carried out by the *Monopolies Commission* and the *Takeover Panel of the Stock Exchange.*

The Monopolies and Mergers Commission seeks to promote competition stressing the need to extend consumer sovereignty, efficiency and enterprise. Since 1980 it has had the authority to make efficiency audits of public sector enterprises.

Types of integration

The growth of a firm, as we have noted, may take place by either of two methods, expansion or integration. The term 'integration' is applied to changes which add new products and processes; the direction of *growth* within the integration may be along one of three routes. A firm may grow *horizontally* by combining with firms which make similar products. It may grow *vertically* by undertaking *manufacturing processes* which are a continuation of those which it already performs. The third route is that of *lateral growth* or *diversification* whereby the firm extends the list of products it already manufactures.

(a)   *Horizontal integration*:   Horizontal integration leaves the range of a firm's activities unchanged. It may take the form of an *extension* of *plant* and increase in output or combination with firms making similar products. Horizontal integration is a common form of growth, as the firm which is successful in one line of business seeks to extend that line. Also this route facilitates the achievement of the two basic motives for growth. If a firm grows by expansion of output, economies of scale are gained which would otherwise be sacrificed if operations were instead widened to new products. Similarly a combination of firms producing different items lacks the strength of a combination of similar firms.

An example is that of a car-manufacturing firm building more production lines or combining with another car manufacturing company.

(b)   *Vertical integration*:   This is growth by moving into another stage of production within the same industry. A firm may extend its process of manufacture backwards towards the *raw materials* or forwards towards the market. Vertical integration tends to be motivated by the desire to eliminate transaction costs, to secure supplies, to improve the distribution network, to gain economies of scale and to nullify increasing entry barriers.

(c) *Lateral integration or diversification*: Lateral integration or diversification is the expansion of a particular firm into an industry with which it was previously unconnected. The motives for diversification can be identified as follows:

- *Uncertainty*: Firms operate under conditions of uncertainty. A highly specialized firm will, in the event of a sharp downturn in the demand for its products, be faced with a serious decline in profits. Firms therefore diversify to guard against this outcome.
- *Product life cycle*: Products go through stages of rapid expansion, maturity and decline, and the onset of maturity or decline in existing products combined with the desire for growth gives a powerful inducement to diversify.
- *Growth*: A firm seeking to grow will often diversify because its existing markets are not expanding quickly enough.

2.4.4 Economies of scale

Large-scale production can reduce the *average cost* per unit because fixed costs are spread over more units. This is known as economies of scale. The economies of large-scale production may be either 'internal' or 'external'.

Internal economies are those which are open to a single factory or a single firm independently of the action of other firms.

External economies are those which are shared by a number of firms or industries when the scale of production in any industry or group of industries increases.

Internal economies

Internal economies can be divided into four main categories:

(a) *Technical economies*: There are a number of kinds of technical economy. Large-scale operations may make greater use of advanced machinery. Also larger machines usually possess greater mechanical advantages. There is often economy in larger machines in the fact that they can generally be operated by a team no larger than is required for a much smaller machine of the same type. Technical economies can also arise from the linking of processes. This produces economies of time, transport costs, fuel etc. One further technical economy of scale is that arising from the fact that more resources can be devoted to research because the cost is borne over more units of output.

(b) *Managerial economies*: The need for management does not increase at the same rate as output. Expansion and production on a large scale also increases opportunities for *specialization*. This specialization is twofold and produces two kinds of managerial economy. First the specialization enabled by large-scale production allows for the *delegation* of routine work and details to subordinates. A second managerial economy arises from *functional specialization*.

(c) *Trading economies*: Advantages can be gained in *buying* and *selling*. Large companies can employ specialist buyers and through the quantity of its purchases it can gain significant *discounts*. Bulk selling also enables savings to be made in distribution costs and advertising.

(d) *Financial economies*:   The large firm has many financial advantages. It has a wider reputation and more influence amongst those who have money to lend or invest. It can borrow from *bankers* upon better *security* and raise *capital* more readily through the issue of *shares* and *debentures* than a small firm. There is a wide and regular *market* for these shares, so that *shareholders* can realize their capital without any of the trouble to which they would be put in a small private concern. Thus the cost of obtaining credit or of raising fresh capital is lower for a large than for a small firm.

External economies

These may be divided into two kinds:

(a) *Economies of concentration*:   The concentration of a number of firms in a particular area facilitates *mutual advantages* through the training of skilled workforces, the provision of better transport facilities etc.

(b) *Economies of information*:   In large industry trade and technical *publications* are issued. Manufacturers are thus saved much independent research which, in a smaller industry, they might be forced to undertake for themselves. It becomes possible also to set up *research associations* which will carry out research work on behalf of individual firms and publish the results for any firm to use.

2.4.5   Diseconomies of scale

Diseconomies of scale exist when the average cost rises with increased production. There are three kinds of diseconomy of scale as follows:

(a) *Technical*:   If a plant reaches its optimum technical size then large *administrative overheads* often result.

(b) *Trading*:   Large-scale production may lead to products becoming *standardized*. The lack of individualism may then reduce consumer choice and lead to lower sales.

(c) *Managerial*:   The increase in size of a firm often results in senior management becoming too remote and losing control. A concomitant of this is a deterioration in *labour relations*.

2.4.6   The small business sector under the Conservative government

The small business sector has expanded since the election of the first Thatcher government in 1979. A number of reasons have been given for this development.

There is an Enterprise Allowance Scheme designed to encourage self-employment and setting up of new business. It provides financial advice and the provision of a £40 per week Government grant during the first year of business.

(a) The Conservative government claims that the expansion of the small business sector is due to the 'enterprise culture' they have created.

The principal government measures designed to encourage small business include the *Business Enterprise Scheme*.

(b) Large numbers of *redundancies* in sizeable firms have increased the number of *unemployed* looking for alternative means of earning a living. Redundancy payments have also provided people with the necessary start-up capital.

(c) There has been a development of *workspaces* which have been leased to budding *entrepreneurs*.

(d) *Tax changes* have been introduced to benefit small business; there is a lower rate of *corporation tax* for small business.

2.4.7 Strengths and weaknesses of the small firm

The major strengths of the small firm lie in its *adaptability* to customer needs: its provision of *individual service* and its ability to offer *variety* of product. Also small retailers may be able to develop a local monopoly as a consequence of limitations in transport of local people without a car.

The central weakness of the small firm is its dependence on a single good or service. Also small firms find it difficult to raise finance in the form of loans, and they are restricted in the means available to them for raising *finance*.

2.4.8 Costs and profits

Costs of production

Cost of production can be defined as the *prices* paid for *factors of production* and the *opportunity cost* attributable to factors already owned.

Factors of production include land, labour, capital etc.

(a) *Fixed and variable costs*: *Fixed costs* are those which do not change with the level of production. *Variable costs* are those which *do* change with the level of output.

(b) *Short run and long run*: The short run is 'a period of time in which at least one factor of production is fixed'. This fixed factor definition means that the level of production in the short run can only be increased by adding more variable factors to the fixed factor. The long run is where all factors of production are considered to be variable.

(c) *Total cost and average cost*: Total cost is obtained by adding fixed costs to variable costs. The average cost is calculated by dividing total cost by total output.

(d) *Diminishing marginal returns*: When a firm increases output in the short run by adding a variable input, such as labour, to a fixed factor, total output initially increases. Eventually, however, *diminishing returns* set in as less efficient labour is recruited and there are limitations imposed by the fixed factor constraint. Therefore, the return from each extra variable factor decreases.

Diminishing returns holds that in any productive process, if some inputs are held fixed while other inputs are increased, then sooner or later the output per variable input will decline. It also implies that after some point each additional unit of a variable input adds less to output than the previous unit did.

(e) *Scale of production*: As production expands, total fixed costs remain unchanged in the short run. However, because they are spread over more units of output average fixed costs fall.

(f) *Marginal cost*: Marginal cost is the extra cost of increasing output by one unit.

2.4.9 Theories of the firm

The traditional theory of the firm assumes that firms aim simply to maximize *profits*. This theory is based on the premise that profit will be maximized where marginal revenue equals marginal cost. Before we examine this theory and others, however, we must define profit.

Profit is the difference between the total *expenses* incurred in producing or acquiring a commodity and the total *revenue* accruing from its sale. Economists distinguish several types of profit.

(a) *Normal profit*: This is the amount of profit needed to keep the entrepreneur in his present activity.
(b) *Abnormal profits*: Those earned above normal profit. Abnormal profits may arise due to a shortage enabling a firm to raise prices and take extra profits.

The profit maximization theory of the firm has been criticized primarily on two accounts. The first objection is that, while profit maximization may appear to be a simple, unambiguous aim in theory, it is not so in practice. The model of a profit-maximizing firm is an owner-managed firm producing only one good, which knows all future cost and revenue streams with certainty. In reality firms are faced with much more complex decisions to be taken in a *dynamic* and *uncertain* environment.

The second objection is that the whole idea of profit maximization is misconceived, because firms may be aiming to do something completely different. This objection to profit maximization rests on the fact that in modern economies the *ownership* of companies is *divorced* from *control*. The alternative theories of the firm arise out of this fact. These alternative theories of the firm can be divided into three categories:

Divorce of ownership from control arises as the day-to-day running is invested in the hands of managers whilst the other functions of the entrepreneur in providing capital and taking a risk are taken by the shareholders.

Another maximizing aim may be that of sales maximization, or growth maximization.

(a) *Managerial*: These theories focus on management as the *decision maker* with a maximizing aim other than profit, but subject to a profit constraint.
(b) *Satisficing*: *Satisficing* theories of the firm project the management with a need to achieve a satisfactory target for at least two major variables i.e. company growth, share price value.
(c) *Behavioural*: Behavioural theories of the firm perceive their objective as describing what happens in firms recognizing the complexities of individuals and groups.

2.4.10 Industrial location

Every industrial establishment has a *location*. Various location theories have been propounded but it can be said that there is no generally acceptable 'location theory' for a number of reasons. First the motives of firms vary; then also different factors vary in importance between industries. Third, the relative importance of factors changes over time.

Localization of industry

Localization is the *concentration* of an *industry* in a particular area. The initial attraction to industry of that area may have been the availability of *energy* supplies or the existence of a *raw material* or a *nodal* situation, as at a major port or junction of routes. Whatever the reason for the initial establishment of industrial enterprise, the very existence of active industry may make the location attractive to other industries.

For example historically the location of the iron and steel industry has been determined by energy supplies and supplies of coal as its raw material.

As *localization* of industry occurs a number of advantages are gained. The area becomes a centre of concentrated earning power, and therefore of *purchasing power*. In other words it becomes a bigger and better market for the consumer goods industries, many of which will be attracted to the location. The labour supply will grow in numbers and in skills which will further enhance the attractions of the location for yet other processes. *Tertiary* services will also expand and specialist financial *institutions* will be established to meet the financial needs of industry. A further advantage of localization lies in the development of *infrastructure*.

These include transport, banking, catering, retail units etc.

As the twentieth century has advanced there has been a trend away from localization. This is due to a general *de-industrialization*, an increasing lack of importance of proximity to raw materials and *industrial dispersion*.

2.4.11 Regional problems

In the nineteenth century, industrial location was resource based, a consequence of which was the localization or concentration of heavy manufacturing industry in the North. Since that time there has been a demise in heavy manufacturing and the emergence of *light industry*. This has been detrimental to the North causing large-scale localized unemployment.

This includes light engineering – electronics, computing etc.

Recent research, by Newcastle University's centre for urban and regional development studies, has led to the computation of a *prosperity index*. The index demonstrates a North–South divide with prosperity concentrated in the south. The index also reveals an urban–rural divide – the poorer parts of the South are urban and the richer areas of the North are rural.

The variables used in computing this prosperity index were latest unemployment rate, recent changes in employment and percentage of households with two cars.

Several regional problems dominate:

(a) *High unemployment*: As heavy manufacturing industry has suffered severe decline in the regions high structural unemployment has resulted, and with it, lower incomes.

(b) *Congestion and overcrowding*: This occurs in regions of growth.

(c) *Inner city decay*: Central districts in a number of large cities have become run down, disused and vandalized.

2.4.12 Regional policy

There are two approaches to regional policy, the *free market* approach and government *intervention*.

The former approach considers that firms should make their own locational decisions without government interference. The priority is therefore given to the private costs and benefits to firms without consideration of social needs, consequences and costs.

The aim of the second approach is to give priority to social considerations. Government intervention in the location decision takes a number of forms as follows:

(a) *Assisted areas*: These are mainly *development areas*, which are areas of high unemployment and declining basic industries.

(b) *Regional planning*: Economic planning councils were established throughout the English regions in 1965 and in 1975 Scottish and Welsh Development Agencies were established.

Government can also influence location decisions by means of a variety of *incentives* and *deterrents*. Incentives are offered to firms to locate in 'problem' areas by means of capital subsidies or grants for plant, and labour subsidies.

Further government intervention has been facilitated by exercising physical controls over planning as follows:

(a) Government contracts are often deliberately placed with firms in depressed areas.

(b) Industrial Development Certificates are needed by firms wishing to locate outside development areas.

(c) Government department offices have been located in development areas.

(d) Improvements have been made to the infrastructure in development areas to attract new firms.

(e) *Enterprise Zones* have been established where firms are less restricted with regard to planning regulations, requests for information, VAT procedures. In addition rates are not levied and a 100 per cent capital allowance was given on business property purchased.

Revision questions

1 Account for the survival and expansion of the small business unit/sector in the UK.

2 Discuss the similarities and differences in the objectives of a public corporation and those of a limited company.

3
Supply and demand

3.1 Topic relationship

An understanding of the principles of *supply* and *demand* is essential at a microeconomic level. *Price* – a fundamental concept of economics – is governed by supply and demand i.e. by *cost* on the one hand and *utility* on the other.

Utility can be defined as the power or degree to which human wants are satisfied.

3.2 Underlying concepts

Supply is the *quantity* that a person or firm wants to sell at a particular price; thus the supply of a good increases if its price increases. The relation between the supply of a good and its price is given by its supply schedule and is represented by a *supply curve*.

Demand is the relationship between consumers' desire to buy a good and price. The nature of this relationship is shaped by a number of factors, the key factor being the amount of pleasure or utility gained from consuming a good.

The forces of demand and supply form the key process in the *price mechanism*. Price is the main characteristic of any *market* and the price mechanism is the means by which the *pattern* of *production* is made to match consumers' *wants*.

Supply and demand are market forces – an important underlying concept is that relating to the nature of the market or condition of the market i.e. the degree of *competition* or *monopoly* within the market. Competition is fundamentally the existence of a *substitute*; monopoly is fundamentally the *absence of substitutes*.

The theory of price mechanism holds that if supply increases, while demand remains constant, prices will fall; if demand increases, while supply remains constant, prices will rise.

In practice there cannot be a situation of perfect competition nor can there be a complete monopoly because there can never be perfect information nor an entire absence of substitutes; instead markets exist at some point between monopoly and perfect competition.

3.3 Points of perspective

Supply and demand are fundamental economic forces which are in operation and by whose operation *resources* are *allocated*. When demand *equals* supply the forces are said to be in *equilibrium*. When a market is in equilibrium, price is such that there are no economic forces working on either the demand or the supply side to change the quantities bought and sold, which are also said, therefore, to be in equilibrium.

As we have noted the *interaction* of supply and demand forms the key process in the price mechanism and it is by the price mechanism that *scarce* resources are allocated among *competing uses* i.e. it provides a solution to the basic economic problem.

3.4   Essential knowledge

3.4.1   *The supply curve of a firm*

The supply curve of a firm varies between the *short run* and the *long run*.

A firm's *supply curve* shows the amount that it produces at each price. As long as the price (which equals *average revenue*) exceeds average *variable* cost, a firm produces the *output* for which *marginal* revenue equals marginal cost. If the price is below its minimum average variable cost, the firm produces nothing. In Figure 3.1, output is zero when the price is below A. The output is B when the price is C and the output is D when the price is E. Therefore the firm's short-run supply curve is its marginal cost curve for all prices shown above A.

The short-run market supply at each price is the sum of the short-run supplies of all firms supplying the market.

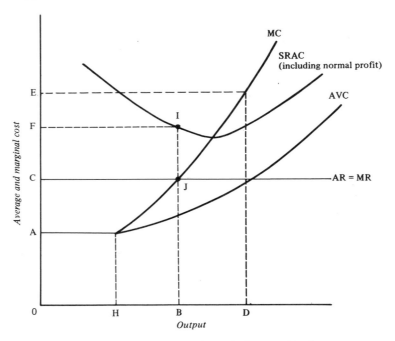

Figure 3.1   *Supply curve in the short run for perfectly competitive firm*

Figure 3.1 illustrates a firm that cannot make a *supernormal* profit when the price is C, because average cost (AC) exceeds average revenue at all outputs. At output B, where marginal revenue equals marginal cost (MC), the firm's *loss* is as small as possible. In the short run a firm cannot avoid paying its *fixed cost*, even if it produces nothing, because it is committed to particular fixed factors.

In the *traditional* theory the *marginal cost* curve also becomes the *supply curve* in the long run. Yet it will not necessarily be upward sloping because AC (and thus MC) can be increasing, constant or decreasing in the long run. The AC was increasing in the short run because of *diminishing returns* caused by the fixed factor assumption. This assumption is relaxed in the long run and so MC (and thus supply) could be downward sloping left to right (if *economies of scale* occur), constant or upward sloping (*diseconomies*).

The supply curve shows how supply depends on price, but supply is also influenced in other ways. The quantity supplied at each price also depends on:

(a) The costs of *factors of production* – if these costs increase, supply is likely to fall because some *suppliers* can no longer make a profit, and so they are likely to go out of business.
(b) The *technology* available to *producers* – supply increases if a new method of production is invented that enables firms to produce more *cheaply*.
(c) The prices of other goods that people and firms could supply instead.
(d) *Random events*, including the weather which affects production in the agricultural and building industries in particular.

3.4.2 The supply curve of an industry

The market supply curve is composed of all the supply curves of the individual producers in the industry. It shows the total amount that people and firms want to supply at each price. (See Table 3.1.)

This can be illustrated as a market supply curve as shown in Figure 3.2.

3.4.3 The elasticity of supply

The *elasticity of supply* of a *commodity* is the *rate* at which the quantity offered for sale *changes* as the price changes. It can be expressed thus:

$$\text{Elasticity of supply} = \frac{\text{Percentage change in quantity offered}}{\text{Percentage change in price}}$$

Table   3.1

Selling price (£)	Quantity supplied (units)		
	Firm X	Firm Y	Industry
0	0	0	0
1	10	11	21
2	18	19	37
3	25	26	51
4	32	33	65
5	39	40	79

Figure 3.2   *The market supply curve*

Supply is said to be *elastic* or *inelastic* as a change in price causes a more than *proportionate* or less than proportionate change in supply respectively.

3.4.4   *Determinants of elasticity of supply*

The elasticity of supply depends on the ability of producers to back away from the market if prices fall, and on their ability and willingness to expand sales if prices rise. Thus elasticity of supply depends on:

Elasticity of supply, therefore, grows with time as the range and quantity of goods increases.

(a)   *Time*:   The response of consumers and producers to a change in price is generally spread over a period of time; some reactions are immediate and some delayed.

(b)   *Characteristics of the production process*:   If the item has a close substitute in production i.e. if the *labour* or equipment used to produce it can be readily switched into the production of another good, then the supply will be elastic.

The same is true of goods that are costly to store.

(c)   *Feasibility and cost of storage*:   Goods that rot quickly must be supplied regardless of price; their elasticity of supply is, therefore, very low.

(d)   *Range of market*:   If the producer is selling in several different markets, his goods are likely to be in elastic supply to any one market; a fall in prices in that market will induce him to sell his goods elsewhere.

(e)   *Range of products*:   If the manufacturer is producing several goods and can switch easily from one to another, then each of his products will be in elastic supply.

3.4.5   *Shifts in supply and movements along the supply curve*

Shifts in the supply curve are caused by a change in the conditions of supply
and consequently the price changes. This can be illustrated by Figures 3.3,
3.4 and 3.5.

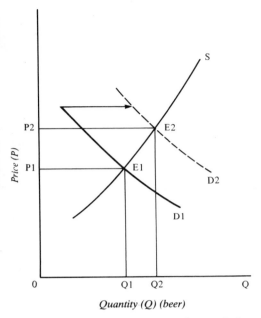

*As tastes move towards beer the demand
curve shifts to D2.*

Figure 3.3   *Supply curve movements, increase in demand*

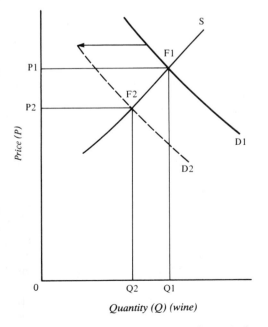

*As a result of the drop in demand for wine
the demand curve shifts to D2.*

Figure 3.4   *Supply curve movements, reduction in demand*

Figures 3.3 and 3.4 show that a change in *tastes* causes the demand for beer to increase and the demand for wine to decrease. As a result more beer is bought, at a higher price. (See Figure 3.3.) Less wine is bought, and the price of wine falls. (See Figure 3.4.) This is a *movement along* the supply curve.

Figure 3.5 shows shifts in the supply curve to the left. Factors causing shifts in the supply curve are:

(a) *Technology*: If there is an improvement in technology, *costs* of *production* will fall. Lower costs will persuade producers to supply more at any particular price, thus the supply curve will shift to the right.

(b) *The cost of inputs*: If the cost of inputs increases the manufacturer will be less willing to produce the good at the previously prevailing price, thus the supply curve will shift to the left.

(c) *Indirect taxes*: The imposition of an *indirect* tax, or a higher rate charged, or lower *subsidies* all make supply at existing prices less *profitable*. The tax will reduce the *profit margin* and thereby the costs of production will be raised indirectly and thus the supply curve will shift to the left.

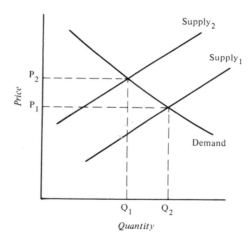

Figure 3.5 *Shifts in supply curve*

3.4.6 Consumer behaviour and demand

The key processes in the *price mechanism* are the forces of demand and supply. Demand is the relationship between a consumer's desire to buy a good and price. This section examines the factors that determine the *shape* of this relationship. The key factor is the amount of pleasure or *utility* gained from consuming a good.

Utility and consumption

Utility cannot be measured in absolute terms: we cannot exactly measure how happy a person is or how much utility he has. Instead measurement of utility is *relative*. Such relative measurement is important for the theory of demand.

The law of diminishing marginal utility can only be proven by examining the reactions of a majority of people in an economy. Such examination reveals that diminishing marginal utility is the consequence of additional consumption i.e. as our consumption of a commodity increases our *satisfaction* with it decreases, we become sated with it. (See Table 3.2.)

It must be noted that timescale plays an important part in this theory. For example, the consumption of a fifth good in one day would give us no increased utility but consumption of a fifth good in one week would give an increase in utility.

Table 3.2

Quantity of goods consumed	Total utility	Marginal utility (gain from one additional unit)
0	0	
1	8	8
2	14	6
3	18	4
4	20	2
5	20	0

Demand and utility

Diminishing marginal utility is reflected in a consumer's willingness to *pay* for goods. As utility gained from consumption of a good falls the consumer will be prepared to pay less for that good. In other words the consumer will only demand more of a commodity at lower prices. (See Table 3.3.)

Table 3.3

Quantity of beer demanded per person per week (pint)	Price per pint (£)	Total utility (utils)	Marginal utility (utils)
1	1.6	200	200
2	0.85	380	180
3	0.70	540	160
4	0.55	680	140
5	0.5	800	120
6	0.45	900	100

The schedule is based on a false idea in that it measures the utility a person gains from consumption in absolute units. The third column measures utility in '*utils*'. Thus a person consuming one good per day experiences four utils of welfare; when consuming two goods per day he experiences seven utils etc.

Marginal utility is the most important feature on the schedule; it is a key concept underlying demand. It can be defined as the additional utility or satisfaction an individual receives from consuming one additional unit of a good or service. Table 3.3 shows that a person's marginal utility decreases as he consumes more. This is called the law of diminishing marginal utility.

We do not know what a 'util' is; rather it is used to make a relative measurement of a person's utility between one state and another.

Figure 3.6 illustrates the relationship between the quantity of beer demanded per week and the price at which it can be bought i.e. it shows that as demand increases prices fall.

More specifically it is essential to grasp that the price of a good does not depend on *total utility* but is a function of *marginal utility*. For example the consumer who consumes four pints of beer per week at 55p per pint must consider the increase in utility he gains from the fourth pint (140 utils) to equal the utility from 55p otherwise he would not buy the fourth pint of beer. Thus the price a consumer is prepared to pay for a good represents the marginal utility which the purchase of the good represents to the consumer.

One can conclude from this that the price of any good depends on the marginal utility of the last *portion* of that good demanded.

For example a person will not buy the fourth pint if it costs more than 55p because the fourth pint only gives 140 utils and those utils are worth no more than 55p.

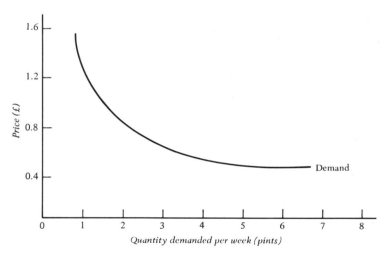

Figure 3.6   *The demand curve*

3.4.7   *Indifference curves*

Economic behaviour involves a choice between *alternatives*. Consumers have a scale of *preference* which shows which *combination* of products they value most highly. Suppose a household has to choose between coffee and tea, the decision it faces can be shown on an indifference curve.

Suppose that the household begins at a point chosen at random in Figure 3.7; say point B where it is consuming two units of coffee and 2 units of tea. To draw the indifference curve through B we may then seek to consider what other combinations of coffee and tea would leave the household equally well off.

The household may inform us that it would just as soon be at point C with four units of tea and one of coffee. In other words, if the household starting at B were asked to give up a unit of coffee in return for 2 units more of tea, it would respond that it is indifferent. Thus the household is indifferent

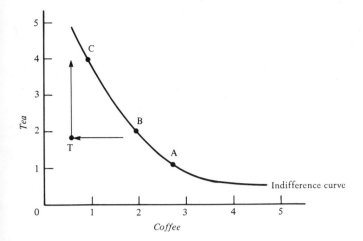

Figure 3.7 *An indifference curve*

Point T in Figure 3·7 is on a lower indifference curve because it gives less coffee but no more tea than point B.

between points B and C; these two points are thus on an indifference curve.

3.4.8 *Elasticity of demand*

Price elasticity of demand

Price elasticity of demand is the measurement of the *degree* to which the quantity of a good demanded *reacts* to changes in its *market price*. It acts primarily as an *indicator* of how total revenue changes when a fall in price brings increased quantity along the demand curve.

The equation expressing elasticity of demand is as follows:

$$\text{Ed} = \frac{\%\ \text{change in quantity demanded}}{\%\ \text{change in price}}$$

In circumstances where the percentage change in price causes a greater percentage change in quantity this is known as elastic demand. A situation of inelastic demand is where the percentage change in price creates a lesser percentage change in quantity.

The five major factors affecting elasticity of demand are as follows:

(a) *Habit*:   Where purchase of a good is determined to some degree by habit, demand tends to be inelastic in face of price change.
(b) *Degree of necessity*:   Demand tends to be inelastic the greater the degree of necessity for a good.
(c) *Substitution*:   There is a greater elasticity of demand for a good if more substitutes are available.
(d) *Time*:   A change in price in a short period of time may have little influence on demand as it often takes some time for all consumers to be aware of the price change.

(e)   *Derived demand*:   A good demanded in order that another good may be consumed is called a derived demand e.g. factors of production.

Income elasticity of demand

Income elasticity of demand measures the change in the demand for a good caused by a change in income and it is expressed as follows:

$$\text{Income elasticity of demand} = \frac{\% \text{ change in quantity demanded}}{\% \text{ change in income}}$$

The concept of income elasticity of demand is less important than that of price elasticity, but it is important as a mechanism for *predicting* how demand will change in the future in response to changes in income.

Cross elasticity of demand

This refers to the *link* between a price change for one good and demand for another. For example, the demand for motor cars may increase if the price of petrol falls dramatically and vice versa.

3.4.9   Conditions of demand

There are a number of conditions of demand:

(a)   *Population*
(b)   *Consumer preferences*
(c)   *Price of substitutes*
(d)   *Income*:   A change in *distribution* of income in which incomes of higher-income groups were reduced by a taxation policy would create a situation of *reduced* demand for goods associated with the high-income groups.

3.4.10   The market mechanism

A market may be defined as 'the totality of all acts of buying and selling a particular good in a given period of time'.

The price mechanism

Price is the main characteristic of any market and the price mechanism is the means by which the pattern of production is made to match consumers' wants. The theory of the 'price mechanism' is as follows. If supply increases, while demand remains *constant*, prices will fall; if demand increases, while supply remains constant, prices will rise. The movements in prices tend to restore the *balance* between supply and demand. If there is an *excess* of supply over demand, or of demand over supply, prices tend to move so as to wipe out the excess and bring supply and demand back into line with one another.

This is described as being in equilibrium.   When the price of a good is such that the amount demanded at that price is equal to the amount supplied at that price, it will then be an '*equilibrium*' price.

Perfect competition

Perfect competition presupposes two conditions: a large number of *competing* sellers and a *perfect* market. A perfect market is one in which buyers have no preferences between the different units of the commodity for sale, sellers are quite *indifferent* to whom they sell, and both buyers and sellers have full *knowledge* of prices in other parts of the market. For competition in a commodity to be perfect, each individual buyer and seller of the commodity must regard the market price as entirely beyond his *control*. Thus prices will not be deliberately held down by buyers *restricting* purchases, nor will prices be deliberately forced higher by sellers restricting output. Each buyer or seller will form his own judgement of the probable course of prices and will treat the price which he anticipates as unaffected by his individual purchases or sales.

As far as the individual firm is concerned, therefore, since it is only one of a very large number of firms in the industry it will assume that nothing which it alone does to adjust its output will have any appreciable effect on the total output of the good and therefore on the unit price. It will thus take the *current* price as given; this price will therefore at all levels of its output measure the relevant marginal '*benefit*'; and this means that the firm will be in equilibrium when it fixes its output so as to *equate* marginal cost and price. At this equilibrium output, however, the firm may in the short period be making either abnormal profits or losses in which case, in the long period, new firms will come into the industry, or some of the existing firms will leave the industry, until the forces of competition have as a result lowered or raised the price to the level which affords each firm no more and no less than '*normal*' profits. This long-run equilibrium situation possesses four apparently desirable characteristics:

(a)   There are no abnormal profits.
(b)   Consumers are getting the good at the lowest possible price consistent with covering costs.
(c)   There is no underuse or overuse of capacity.
(d)   Since price is equal to marginal cost, the allocation problem is being solved in the best possible manner.

Monopoly

Perfect competition where there are many sellers is at one end of the market spectrum; at the other end is monopoly with only one seller, i.e. a single supplier of the good. Firms are not free to enter the market, and the single firm can influence the price in the market.

In the real world we never find monopoly undiluted by competition. Competition is fundamentally the existence of a substitute; monopoly is fundamentally the absence of substitutes. There can never be an entire absence of substitutes however, for so long as *purchasing power* is limited, everything on which money might be spent is in a sense a substitute for everything which is actually bought.

Under perfect competition, the individual firm is a *price taker* – it cannot alter the price of the product by altering its own output. Under a form of monopoly the individual firm is, up to a point, a *price maker* – it *can* alter the price of its product by altering its own output. Under these circumstances, marginal cost will no longer be equal to the unit price at which the relevant output can be sold, but will be less than this price. It can be shown to follow from this that if a pure *monopolist* takes over a competitive industry he will restrict his output below, and raise his price above, the competitive level. Under pure monopoly we can, therefore, find the following characteristics:

(a)   *Abnormal* profits may be received.
(b)   Consumers pay more for the good and get less of it than under pure competition.
(c)   There will probably be either *underuse* or *overuse* of capacity.
(d)   Price is greater than marginal cost, which means that resources are probably being *misallocated*.

Markets between monopoly and perfect competition
There are two basic characteristics of monopolistic competition as follows:

(a)   There are many firms, each of which has some market influence, but none of which is very much larger than the average firm.
(b)   New firms are free to enter the market, and existing firms are free to leave the market.

An *oligopoly* is a market dominated by a *few* sellers who operate without any agreements or understandings between them. Each firm, therefore, has an interest in restricting production for fear of forcing down prices; or alternatively, each firm will have an interest in refraining from cutting prices. Frequently oligopoly is combined with *specialization* within the market.

A *monopsony* is a market with a single buyer. In reality there are few cases in which monopsony occurs in its pure form. There is more likely to be a small group of buyers.

Imperfect competition
Imperfect competition exists when any buyer or any seller is able to influence the price. Under imperfect competition the price will be above the marginal cost of production.

There are a number of reasons for imperfect markets. Imperfection arises out of lack of information; buyers and sellers may be ill-informed about the terms on which dealings are proceeding elsewhere. Also there are preferences due to the different *suitability* of competing goods for the purposes of different buyers. Finally, the market may be imperfect because of preferences which do not originate in real differences between the products of each seller but in fancied differences or in habit.

3.4.11   *Government policy and legislation*

Since 1946, the British Government has been increasingly involved in vetting the operation of markets in the UK. The major legislation aimed at this is as follows:

(a) *Monopolies and Restrictive Practices Act 1948*:   This was the first major legislation; it was *investigatory* and concerned with exposure rather than *punitive* reprisal. It set up the Monopolies Commission with power to investigate and report on monopolies.

(b) *Restrictive Trade Practices Act 1956*:   This Act separated the investigation of restrictive practices from that of monopoly. Restrictive practices were to be dealt with through a new 'High Court', whose decisions were binding, called the Restrictive Practices Court, while monopolies were to be dealt with by a newly constituted commission.

(c) *The Monopolies and Mergers Act 1965*:   This Act injected new life into the Monopolies Commission which had, since 1956, been left only with the task of examining single-firm monopolies. The DTI now had the power to refer *mergers* and proposed mergers to the Monopolies Commission for examination and consideration as to whether they were in the public interest.

(d) *The Fair Trading Act 1973*:   This set out to strengthen and improve the effectiveness of *existing* controls. It appointed a *Director of Fair Trading* to oversee the government's competition and consumer *protection* policies, and to keep under constant review all kinds of *commercial* activity.

(e) *Competition Act 1980*:   This established a new 'competition reference' procedure, with the Office of Fair Trading investigating *anti-competitive* activities, which might restrict, distort or prevent competition.

Any firm controlling at least one quarter of the market with assets exceeding £30 million and referred by the OFT will be investigated by the Monopolies and Mergers Commission (MMC). The MMC seeks to promote competition and stresses the need to extend consumer *sovereignty*, *efficiency*, and *enterprise*. At the same time it recognizes the benefits which are gained through large-scale enterprise from economies of scale and accepts that abnormal profits are a justifiable *reward* for *research*, *development* and *risk-taking*. In addition since 1980 the MMC has had the authority to make efficiency *audits* of public sector enterprises.

The Conservative government's philosophy of free market has changed the brief of the MMC towards extending competition rather than stopping mergers, and investigating contentious cases where 'new issues' are highlighted.

Revision questions

1   Trace the consequences of an increase in the demand for and price of X on the demand for and price of Y, for goods:
  (a)   In joint demand
  (b)   In joint supply

2   British Rail would not change its prices until it had considered the number of passengers who might change to using another form of transport as a result. Provide definitions of price elasticity of demand, income elasticity of demand and cross elasticity of demand and then explain why these would be of importance to British Rail in their decision.

3   Outline the factors which may have an impact on the price of consumer durables.

4
Labour

4.1   Topic relationship

Population is an integral part of economic study as population provides the *labour* force, and changes in population influence *demand* and *supply* patterns.

The *structure* of the population in terms of *age*, *sex* and *geographical distribution* has important economic ramifications; the *size* of each *category* will determine the *resources* available for *production* and the pattern of *consumption* needs. *Age distribution* crucially affects the size of the labour force.

The *non-workers* within the working age group are dependent upon the working population to produce the *goods* and *services* they need to sustain them. If this percentage increases there will be a need for greater *productivity* from those in work, and more *taxation*, unless there is rapid *economic growth*.

4.2   Underlying concepts

A study of population involves coming to terms with aspects such as size, structure, growth, distribution etc. and viewing population as an economic resource.

As an economic resource population is described as '*labour*'. Labour forms the human element in *production* – the physical, mental and emotional input of human beings into the production *process*. A basic underlying economic concept of labour is that of the *price* of labour i.e. *wages*. The price is determined by supply and demand. *Disequilibrium* in supply and demand is a major factor in creating unemployment.

The *political/economic organization* of labour is undertaken by trade *unions*. The basic function of trade unions is that of *collective bargaining* – i.e. *negotiating* pay levels.

One of the economic consequences of the efforts of the population or labour force in the production process is measured in terms of the *standard of living*. This is expressed or measured in terms of *national income*, which is the total *monetary value* of the goods and services produced by a country's resources over a given period of time. Such a *quantitative* measurement leaves room for the concept of increase or *growth*. *Gross domestic product* (GDP) is the most common measure of economic performance.

The labour force or working population consists of people in employment and those seeking employment.

The price of labour is the amount of wage paid by an employer to an employee for his input/work.

The chapter also indicates that growth cannot be measured or understood purely in monetary terms.

4.3   Points of perspective

The population of the UK has *stabilized* at about 56 million during the last quarter of a century. The *rate* of growth has declined with the decline in *natural increase*; only during the decade 1955–1965 has there been a rapid population growth this century. There has been a significant *migration* from Britain during this century – excepting the period 1931–1961. Since 1961 many *emigrants* have been from the professional middle classes and skilled working class – known as 'the *brain drain*'.

Significant changes in the labour force have occurred in the 1980s. There has been an increase in the number of *self-employed*, 2.6 million in 1986 compared with 1.6 million in 1955 – the largest part of that increase taking place since 1980. There has been an increase in the number of *part-timers*; in 1985, 5 million people worked less than thirty hours a week. There has also been a significant increase in *female* employment, women accounting for two-thirds of the part-time employed workforce in 1986, compared with half in 1966. The working week has also shortened, and hours of working tend to be more flexible.

A crude rate is calculated by dividing the number of births, or deaths or marriages by the total population. The crude rates of natural increase are calculated by subtracting crude death rates from crude birth rates.

4.4   Essential knowledge

4.4.1   *Unemployment*

Unemployment can be regarded as the major economic problem of the 1980s, standing at over 3 million. The unemployment of the 1980s manifests several characteristics as follows:

(a)   *Uneven age distribution*:   Unemployment has fallen mainly on men over fifty-five and on young people under twenty-five.

(b)   *Ethnic minorities*:   The rate of unemployment amongst the young of ethnic minorities is usually twice that of white people.

(c)   *Manual workers*:   *Deindustrialization* and the introduction of new *technology* have reduced the need for labour *intensive* activity.

(d)   *Unemployment* has fallen more on those engaged in *manufacturing* than those in *service* industries.

The costs of unemployment are far-reaching. Pure economic costs are evident in the fact that unemployment means an *underutilization* of resources, and also the *financial* cost is quite high as the unemployed do not pay *income tax* and also qualify for a variety of benefits so that each unemployed person costs the government approximately £6,000 per year. But the costs extend beyond the purely economic, as there are significant *social* costs associated with unemployment including deteriorating *health*, rise in *suicides*, increase in *crime* etc. which in turn create costs in terms of higher spending on health, police, training schemes etc.

Income tax is a tax on income in proportion to amount earned.

For example a change in the pattern of demand from cotton to man-made fibres created heavy unemployment in the Lancashire cotton mills; similarly the change in production methods in the printing industry, with the introduction of new technology has produced unemployment.

We can identify different types of unemployment as follows:

(a)   *Structural*:   This type of unemployment is usually 'long term'. It arises due to a change in the pattern of demand, or a significant change in production methods.

For example ski-instructors are less needed during the summer months.

(b) *Seasonal*:   Some occupations experience large fluctuations in demand for their service during a year.

(c) *Frictional (search)*:   This type of unemployment occurs when a worker leaves one job and is about to start another.

(d) *Cyclical*:   The economy tends to experience variations in demand with *fluctuations* in economic growth. A slump in demand will foster an increase in unemployment.

Monetarist school of economics is so called because of its belief that too fast a growth in the supply of money is the invariable cause of inflation and monetary control its only effective cure.

(e) *Voluntary*:   This type of unemployment has largely been defined by the *monetarist* school of economics. This type of unemployment is said to occur when people are unwilling to work at existing wage rates.

A lack of demand for goods and services.

The causes of unemployment are various and wide-ranging but can be broadly divided into demand and supply factors. A 'demand factor' is that of demand *deficiency*. The fall in demand which has contributed to Britain's unemployment was both national and international, stemming largely from the oil price crisis 1973–74. Here funds were *transferred* to oil producers but these did not find their way back to the *developed* economies through demand for their goods, *trade* consequently declined and *redundancies* increased.

Supply factors are quite numerous. The activities of *trade unions* in pressing for higher wages and in resisting improvements in *efficiency* have, according to some observers, priced workers out of jobs, and contributed to rising costs, lower sales and less employment. Another supply factor

It has been suggested that the 'high' benefits encourage voluntary unemployment.

identified by some economists is that of high benefits.

Many economists argue that *national insurance* contributions have deterred firms from *recruitment* as they act as a *payroll tax* for employers.

Finally the increase in working population has meant that employment must rise by 1 per cent per year just to absorb the increase in size of the *working population*.

4.4.2   *Wages and trade unions*

Factors of production

There are three major resources required for production:

(a) *Capital*:   Initially a company will need capital to start its operations; it will then require further finance to continue operations. This may be in the form of *profits*, finance from the selling of shares or loans. This is known as *capital finance*. The capital finance will then be used to acquire '*real capital*'.

Plant machinery and perhaps intangible assets such as patent rights.

(b) *Land*:   This will be needed for the construction of factories, offices etc. The land may be bought or gained on *leasehold*. The advantage of buying the land is that there is a once-and-for-all payment and hence rent will not form part of production costs.

Whereby rent must be paid to the owner.

(c) *Labour*:   Age, skill and sex are important elements in the production factor of labour. Certain jobs require a high level of skill, in which case few people will be qualified to perform that job. It may be that the necessary skill is only acquired with experience and therefore an older *workforce* will be needed. Other tasks, however, may require a youthful workforce. It must be noted that legislation affects employment practices.

The Sex and Race Discrimination Acts respectively legislate against discrimination in recruitment, training and payment on grounds of sex or race.

4.4.3 The price of labour

The wage an employer pays to his employee is, in effect, the price of labour. The price of labour is determined by supply and demand. If there is a shortage of, and high demand for, a particular skill the worker with that skill will receive a high wage.

The demand for labour is a derived demand i.e. its demand depends upon the demand for the commodity it is engaged in producing.

Table 4.1 and Figure 4.1 show the derivation of demand curves. The *ARP* curve shows the value of the average production of each worker at various employment levels and the *MRP curve* shows the amount of revenue gained from the sale of goods produced by an extra unit of labour. Each good is sold at £2.50.

The average revenue product and marginal revenue product can be graphed as shown in Figure 4.1.

The ARP is the revenue generated by the sale of the average product. The Marginal Revenue Product (MRP) is the revenue gained through selling the product gained from employing the last additional worker.

Table 4.1

Number of men (a)	Total units produced (b)	Average units produced per man (c)	Marginal product (physical) (d)	Average revenue product (c)* £2.50	Marginal revenue product (d)* £2.50
1	14	14	14	35	35
2	32	16	18	40	45
3	57	19	25	47.5	62.5
4	84	21	27	52.5	67.5
5	115	23	31	57.5	77.5
6	132	22	27	55	67.5
7	147	21	15	52.5	37.5
8	155	19.4	8	48.5	20
9	160	17.8	5	44.5	12.5

*Price

Figure 4.1 shows that when the MRP curve is below the ARP curve it is the same as the *demand curve*. For example, if the company employed a fifth man he would increase revenue by £77.50 and the company should consequently be willing to pay him £77.50. A sixth man would, however, only add £67.50 and therefore he would receive no more than £67.50. If there is perfect competition in the labour market and all workers who perform the same task are paid the same wage then the MRP curve is also the demand curve as it shows how many men a company will have at a certain wage rate.

Labour is a *derived* demand and therefore if the demand for the final product is *elastic* so also will be the demand for labour. Yet, if labour costs form only a small part of the overall cost of the finished product the elasticity of demand for the labour will be reduced. For example, if labour

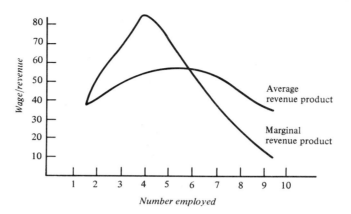

Figure 4.1   *Demand curve for labour*

costs rise by 20 per cent yet only form 5 per cent of total costs there will be an increase of only 1 per cent in the price of the finished product. Such a small change in the price of a product will hardly affect demand and therefore the elasticity of demand for labour will be reduced.

As the demand curve for labour rises higher so also will the wages of the workers. The demand curve for labour is determined by *marginal physical product* multiplied by price and therefore any alteration of either of these two *determinants* will change the nature of the demand curve.

Two factors determine the marginal physical product of labour. The first is the resources available to that labour. For example, the 100th worker in an economy operating on one acre of land will add less to total output than his opposite number in an economy with fifty acres of land because diminishing returns to the fixed factor, land, will be more pronounced.

The second factor determining marginal physical product of labour is technical expertise, and the quality of *management*. In an economy using *advanced technology* and with good management, the worker will produce more than his counterpart in an economy operating with poor machinery under poor management. In both cases the workers in the less productive economies may be working just as hard as those in the more productive economies but conditions are not conducive to their achieving high levels of *output*. (See Figure 4.2.)

That is unproductive fixed factors.

The use of high technology will increase output levels but in order to maximize its effectiveness it needs to be large in relation to the labour force. For example if an economy has thirty high-technology machines and thirty workers (30H), each worker will have a high productivity and, consequently, high wages. If that economy employed 500 workers the marginal productivity of the 500th worker would be small and the wage rate would, therefore, be low.

Economy B in Figure 4.2.

Such a situation had existed in the oil industry, but in the steel industry an oversupplying of world markets has kept prices low and consequently steel workers' wages are relatively low.

The final price of a good is the second determinant of the *height* of the demand curve. For example, if the price of the *final goods* is high the MRP curve and thus the demand curve would be high and the wage rates of the workers would be increased.

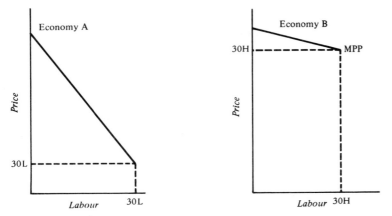

Figure 4.2   *The height of the demand curve*

MPP *is the marginal physical product i.e. the actual number of goods produced by the last additional worker.*

Figure 4.2 shows economy A with low productivity rates. The marginal physical product of the thirtieth labourer is low, hence the wage (P) is small. In Economy B the thirtieth labourer produces much more and receives a higher wage.

A limited *supply* of labour usually forces an increase in wage rates. Yet, if fewer hours are worked and output falls then depending on the *demand curve* the total *earnings* of workers will also fall unless the *wage rate* per hour is increased.

4.4.4   The supply of labour

When a worker is receiving high wages but has little *leisure* he will tend to *substitute* leisure for extra *income*. This is a dimension of *diminishing marginal utility* which often occurs in advanced economies.

The *mobility* of labour is the most important determinant of the supply of labour to various industries. Labour tends to be immobile in geographical terms, also in *occupational* terms, and it is immobile with regard to moving within an industry. This immobility is caused by a number of factors including a lack of training, housing, pension plans and trade union protection.

4.4.5   Determination of the wage rate

The wage rate is largely determined by *elasticity* of the labour supply i.e. the amount by which wage rates need to increase to attract more workers.

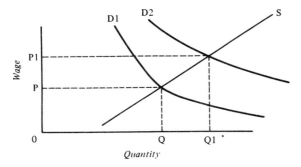

Figure 4.3   *Wage rate with elastic supply*

In low-skilled *occupations* the labour supply is usually elastic, that is, there is a ready supply of labour available to meet any increased demands. As a consequence the wage rate need only increase minimally to attract the extra labour. (See Figure 4.3.)

Where labour supply is inelastic, as tends to be the case in highly skilled occupations, an increase in demand will increase wage rates. (See Figure 4.4.)

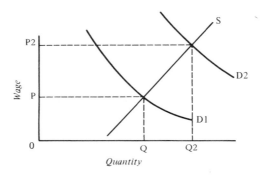

Figure 4.4   *Wage rate with inelastic supply*

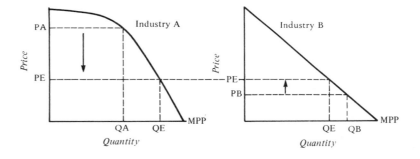

Figure 4.5   *Industry wage differentials*

4.4.6   *Wage differentials*

Wage *differentials* are created by inelasticities of supply and/or non-monetary rewards. Inelasticity of supply causes wage differentials as shown in Figure 4.5.

Figure 4.5 illustrates two industries with different demand curves. If the labour supply was perfectly *elastic* the increase in supply of labour to industry A with the simultaneous decrease in supply to industry B would eradicate the wage differential.

Labour supply is, however, inelastic. A consequence of this inelasticity is that different demands for different jobs will cause differences in wage rates. The sheet metal worker cannot work as a lawyer and any differential in wages between the two will not be wiped out by an increase in supply.

That is if the workers could move freely between industries.

That is not all workers can do all jobs.

Differentials are also caused by *non-monetary rewards*. In effect this is a situation where those in lower-paid jobs are prepared to see those in different occupations earn more because they see in work of others certain non-monetary disadvantages or because they are satisfied with their own occupation because of non-monetary advantages they gain from it.

4.4.7 Trade unions

The emergence of trade unions in all advanced *capitalist* societies suggests that there are strong forces in the labour market which give rise to such *institutions*. Unions in Britain have their roots in the seventeenth and eighteenth centuries when a substantial and permanent class of wage earners began to emerge. The unions were initially confined to *manual* wage earners but in the present century they have extended to virtually all sections of the labour force.

The major concern of trade unions is to increase the wages of their members, although we need to qualify this. The aims of unions are often broad and subject to change. Unions sometimes show an active concern with *political* issues well outside those which immediately affect the interests of their members. It is also evident that unions are concerned with many aspects of jobs other than wages.

Unions are also interested in the pace of work, the level of output, hours and holiday arrangements, safety, recruitment and training.

4.4.8 Collective bargaining

Collective bargaining involves unions and employers primarily *negotiating* pay levels. This may take place on a *national* or *local* level. But it is also more wide-ranging than this. The pay of many employees, especially manual workers, is made up of numerous small payments in addition to the *basic wage*. There may be *supplementary* payments for *overtime*, *shift working* or '*dirty*' conditions; there may also be various fringe *benefits*. In addition to bargaining over pay, the negotiators usually deal with a whole range of issues such as hours of work, discipline, productivity, manning arrangements, training and education, and shift and holiday arrangements.

The power of unions in collective bargaining is determined by a number of factors.

(a) The most important factor is the elasticity of demand for labour. Where this is relatively inelastic unions are able to exercise greater power, because higher wages will have a smaller adverse effect on employment.

(b) A second source of bargaining strength is the coverage of union *membership*. Where membership is higher, sanctions against the employer are likely to be more powerful. The union's ability to *recruit* and *organize* workers thus becomes important.

(c) A third factor which determines bargaining power is the existence of *external* constraints. For example, if the government is trying to reduce the rate of increase of money wages, using an *incomes policy*,

Incomes policies may take the form of direct controls or freezes on wages, salaries, prices and profits, or of taxes on increases in any of these above a norm.

then it may be more difficult to secure wage increases. In some cases employers may be willing to concede union demands but are held back by government *restrictions*. Under these circumstances the union has to direct pressure against the government rather than the employer. Another external factor is the state of *'public sympathy'* for the union's claim.

4.4.9   National income and the standard of living

National income is the *total value* of the goods and services produced by a country's resources over a given period of time, normally one year. It is the *monetary value* of the output produced from a nation's resources. National income as such is used as a measure of a nation's *standard of living*.

The measure of *total output* which an economist decides to use will therefore depend on the particular context for which the measure is required. The measures which are most often used are: *gross domestic product*, *gross national product*, and *capital consumption*.

GDP *measured at market prices is a measure of gross final output at the prices actually paid in the marketplace. GDP at factor cost removes the effect of taxes or subsidies from the prices of certain goods.*

(a)   *Gross domestic product (GDP)*:   This is the value of the output produced within the UK during a period of time. It can be measured at *market prices* and at *factor cost*.

Includes income earned abroad by British residents and companies.

(b)   *Gross national product (GNP)*:   This is the value of the output produced, or incomes earned, by all British *residents* in a year.

(c)   *Capital consumption*:   The nation's capital assets *depreciate* with use and the deduction for this depreciation is termed capital consumption. This is deducted from GNP to get national income.

Calculation of national income
Three methods are used to calculate the value of national income.

This excludes expenditure on raw materials and wholesale products.

(a)   *Expenditure*:   This measures national income by *totalling* expenditure on goods, services and investment by consumers and government. It includes spending on *exports* and deducts expenditure on *imports*. The calculation is concerned with expenditure on final output. *Transfer payments* are deleted from government spending because they are a transfer from taxpayers to recipients via government. Also, indirect taxes are deducted and subsidies added because they artificially change market prices, upwards and downwards respectively.

Transfer payments include things like public pensions and unemployment benefits. Essentially such transfers merely reshuffle income from one group in society to another.

(b)   *Income*:   This measures the income received by the owners of resources for their productive activity. The share of income from employment accounts for over two-thirds of the total and the share attributable to self-employment is increasing. In both cases the gross value of the factor rewards is included and tax and national insurance contributions are ignored because they do not affect the value of the output produced.

(c)   *Output*:   This measures the value of production in each industrial sector. *Double counting* is avoided by taking the value added at each stage of production.

The use of national income statistics

The difficulties involved in the measurement of national income make it at best only a sophisticated *estimate*. National income *statistics* reveal an increase in real national income per head over time but within this it should be remembered that the *tax burden* has increased; that there are significant *regional* variations in income and cost of living and that a change in income distribution might make a few considerably better off and the vast majority marginally worse off.

In comparing the national income of two different economies it must also be noted that there are two underlying differences affecting all others. First, *cultural* differences mean that the way of life will place different values on different *goods* and *services*. Second, the accuracy of the *data* will vary in quality and quantity. For instance, items recorded in one economy may not be included in another country's calculations. In addition *geographical differences*, *political factors*, *social differences*, different *inflation rates* etc. will all restrict valid comparison of national income. Consequently comparison is usually made using selected items which feature in most economies.

For example consumer durables, divorce rates, doctors, participants in higher education.

4.4.10 Economic growth

GDP is the most common measure of economic *growth*, when calculated at *constant prices*. Britain's economic growth has been relatively slow during this century for a number of reasons:

(a) *Structural problems*: A large public sector is argued by some to stunt growth as it is too large, inefficient and produces '*non-marketable*' goods.

(b) *Mismanagement*: Political motives create a series of stop-go economic policies which do not facilitate economic growth.

(c) *Low investment levels*: The small percentage of national income allocated to investment in Britain is given as a cause of low growth by many. Investment has failed to expand in the 1980s because of high real interest rates, a lack of finance and a lack of confidence and *uncertainty* regarding the future of the economy.

Economic growth cannot be equated solely with increased economic *welfare*. The costs of economic growth are becoming more apparent. These range from *social costs* to overconsumption of *irreplaceable* resources, and the development of 'undesirable attitudes' arising out of a changing lifestyle which is *depersonalized* and consumer orientated. In addition, a further concern regarding growth is that its benefits may not be fairly distributed.

For example pollution, acid rain, congestion.

4.4.11 The circular flow of income

The *circular flow* of income refers to the movement of money between different groups in an economy. The basic model of the circular flow of income is based on three assumptions:

(a) No government intervention.

(b) No foreign trade.

(c) That the economy consists of two sectors only: (i) households, (ii) firms.

Firms produce all goods and services, *households* consume those goods produced, and receive payment by offering their labour to firms.

On a more complex level of the model, households may save in addition to consuming. This saving may be invested in firms to enable further production. If the assumption of 'no government intervention' is dropped then it can be counted as a producer and a consumer. In order to obtain funds it will tax, thereby influencing the consumption behaviour of households and the production patterns of firms.

The flow of income becomes yet more complicated when overseas trade is introduced. Money leaves the country as payment for foreign goods but extra income is gained when domestic firms make foreign sales.

Revision questions

1 (a) Define gross domestic product and gross national product.

   (b) What difficulties arise in using gross national product per head to compare international standards of living?

2 What is meant by:

   (a) The immobility of labour?

   (b) Changes in the structure of industry?

   (c) The location of industry.

   How are these related?

3 Provide an outline of the traditional theory of wage determination and the likely effects of unionization on wage rates. Also outline the course of action a union might take in the face of continuing wage role discrimination.

4 Identify and outline the main types of unemployment and the demand and supply factors which contribute to the unemployment.

5
Money and banking

5.1 Topic relationship

The institutions, concepts and relationships in this chapter link with many other ideas in economics. An understanding of the principles of *demand and supply* and *market* activities is essential at a microeconomic level, so that changes in the price of financial assets, and the rate of interest, can be understood. Furthermore, you need to remember that *consumer behaviour* is influenced by the cost and availability of credit while suppliers, too, need to consider such matters when setting *prices* and determining *profit* margins. Similarly, the rate of inflation will influence *production*, planning and *investment*.

However, this chapter relates rather more to macroeconomic issues. The main economic objectives of governments are deeply involved in this chapter. For instance, an awareness of inflation is needed in order to discuss *living standards*, *British trade* and *economic growth*. The operation of the financial sector and the central role of interest rates need to be fully understood so that *budgetary policy* and *public sector borrowing* can be followed. The determination of money supply and the effects of its growth require comprehension in order properly to outline the *monetarist* theory and the *unemployment–inflation* relationship. The role of the central bank in *monetary* policy, *National debt* management and *exchange rate* policy are other important economic relationships in this chapter.

5.2 Underlying concepts

Money can be defined as 'anything that is acceptable to its users in an economic system'. It enables values to be established. The *value* of something when set by money is usually based largely on the cost of production, and reflects relative scarcity. Money facilitates *exchange* between buyers and sellers. *Trade* was limited by the deficiencies of *barter* before money forms were created. The development of money via gold and paper money to *token money* and *credit* has become increasingly reliant on *trust* and *acceptability*.

There are also *near-money* and *money substitutes*. Near-money refers to facilities such as building society *deposits* which are popularly treated as 'money' but do not perform the textbook functions purely. A credit card is termed a money substitute because it does not perform all of the functions expected of money. Another term 'hot money' is used to describe funds which are frequently moved between world financial centres.

We assume the private sector of the British mixed economy, here.

A distinction could be made between actual and projected rates of inflation – see discounted cash flow.

Economic growth, balance of payments, inflation, unemployment and (maybe) redistribution of income and wealth.

There is not one, but many interest rates in the economy in practice.

The main functions (see later) are a medium of exchange, a unit of account and a store of value. Credit cards do not perform the latter.

This is done to gain the benefit of interest rate and exchange rate changes.

Interest is usually calculated as a percentage rate. For instance, a return of £15 on a loan of £150 for one year gives a 10 per cent rate of interest.

In the above example, the nominal rate is 10 per cent. If the annual inflation is 5 per cent then the real rate of interest is 4 per cent. In practice the net return is even lower because income tax is paid on the income received.

The liquidity and profitability of lending tend to be inversely related.

Compare the rate of interest received on bank and building society deposits.

Operations in the money market are classed as 'wholesale banking' while high street banking activities are classified as 'retail banking'.

A bullish market.

The 'single capacity' of one market-maker has replaced the 'dual capacity' of broker and jobber.

Shares or 'equities' are distinct from loan capital where companies borrow from outsiders.

Interest is the return received by the lender of money and the charge placed on borrowers. A distinction can be made between real and nominal rates of interest. The *nominal* rate is the percentage return whereas the *real* rate allows for inflation. Any rate of interest depends upon the *liquidity* and the *risk* of the lending. A loan which is very liquid, such as a bank deposit which can be quickly transformed into cash, will tend to earn a relatively low rate of return. Conversely, high-risk loans earn higher rates of interest. The *time* period involved also affects the interest return. For example, short-term loans usually receive lower rates of interest than similar long-term loans. There are also differences in the interest rates between different financial institutions, when each is attracting deposits and offering similar loans. This is *competition*. These financial institutions are *financial intermediaries* who transfer money from savers to borrowers. There is increasingly more *money-broking* in modern financial markets as bankers move deposits of money and foreign currency between institutions in the money market, with the objective of maximizing their returns.

Capital gain is another motive for holding assets rather than money. Many speculators buy shares in the anticipation of a price rise, which will enable them to sell at a profit; rather than to gain income via the dividend paid. The increased *competition* on the Stock Exchange since the 'Big Bang' has lowered commissions and thus the profits of *market-makers*. These dealers in stocks and shares have replaced stockbrokers and jobbers. Most of the City's financial venues, such as Stock Exchange and Lloyd's are *self-regulating*, with their own rules and disciplinary procedures.

It is possible to make capital gains by holding foreign currencies. There

Clearing banks' average % 1987

Liabilities		Assets	
Deposit accounts	32.9	Cash in tills	0.2
Current accounts	20.6	Balance at Bank of England	0.9
		Money at call	1.6
Foreign currency deposits	32.0	Treasury and other bills	0.9
Capital plus other items	14.5	Market loans	17.0
		Special deposits	–
		Investments	3.1
		Advances	38.7
		Foreign currency loans	37.6
	100.0%		100.0%

Figure 5.1   *Bank balance sheet*

are 'spot' and 'forward' markets for foreign currencies and many primary commodities e.g. zinc. A spot price is the current price whereas forward prices enable traders and speculators to buy something at a future date, say three months ahead, at a price decided now. Trading in futures can be used as a hedge against *inflation* or deflation.

A distinction needs to be made between *bills* and *bonds*. Bills are short-term loans whereas bonds are medium- and long-term assets. *Treasury bills* are ninety-one-day loans to the government and the rate of interest is calculated on the difference between the buying and selling price. *Commercial bills* are effectively loans to traders by financial intermediaries. Bonds are issued by the government at varying lengths of maturity.

A £5,000 bill bought for £4,800 yields 16 per cent interest ($\frac{200}{4800} \times 100 \times \frac{12}{3}$)

Bills and bonds both feature as *assets* on the balance sheet of the banks. The main liabilities of the banks are their deposit and current account holdings. The other assets and bank liabilities are shown in Figure 5.1.

5.3   Points of perspective

This chapter is centred on the heart of *capitalism* in the private sector. Nevertheless, the individuals and institutions are subject to *government interference* and pressure. Conservative governments tend to trust city institutions to *self-regulate* whereas the Labour Party argues for stricter laws and governmental controls. *Political* factors also influence activity in the financial markets e.g. the anticipation of a Labour Party election victory causing share prices to fall.

The nature of money and banking has rapidly changed, particularly in the last quarter of the twentieth century. At a simple level the *names* of the monetary instruments have changed. The 'official rate of interest' in the money market has been bank rate 1945–71, minimum lending rate 1971–81 and unnamed since 1981. Furthermore, the *services* offered by banks have progressed and the speed and accuracy of processing have improved with the application of technology.

Examples such as budget account, credit cards, high interest cheque accounts.

The development of Electronic Funds Transfer at Point of Sale (EFTPoS).

The operation of the financial system has been subject to frequent scrutiny and reform proposals. The Radcliffe Report 1959 proposed an emphasis on liquidity yet the changes of the 1980s saw a return to monetary base. However, the Competition and Credit Control 1971 Paper's emphasis on competition has been furthered by the October 1986 Stock Exchange changes. However, the main innovation has been the institution of money supply as a major economic target, for government monetary policy. Until the emergence of monetarism in the late 1970s, governments were not very concerned about the quantity of money in an economy. The monetarist belief is that inflation can be controlled by manipulating the supply of money, although there is an eighteen-month time lag. As a result in 1980 the Conservative government adopted the medium-term financial strategy (MTFS) which outlined target ranges for monetary growth in succeeding years. These were revised in subsequent years and effectively abandoned in 1986, when inflation had been reduced to 3 per cent.

The ending of fixed rate commissions and the introduction of more foreign dealers.

5.4   Essential knowledge

5.4.1. *Functions of money*

Money needs to be *acceptable* in order to perform its functions in a modern economy. Modern forms of money, such as coins, cheques and credit cards, are also *durable*, *divisible* and *portable*. Nowadays, the quantity of money in society is largely controlled by the main clearing banks and the Bank of England so that its relative *scarcity* can keep it valuable. Prior to the 1844 Bank Charter Act, note issue was not controlled and this caused imprudent lending and subsequent bank failures. This, together with the lack of *uniformity* between the money of different banks, undermined the acceptability of the money. Modern money is no longer backed by *gold* and is *token* money. About 90 per cent of modern money is composed of notional sums in people's bank accounts, upon which claims for payment can be made.

The melted down value of a 20p coin is about 2p worth of metal.

By cheque, credit card, etc.

The above qualities enable money to perform its main functions:

(a) *A medium of exchange*:   Money enables buyers and sellers to trade without the need for barter. It allows people to buy goods and services when and how they want.

Barter was inefficient because some goods were indivisible, rates of exchange were not fixed and the wants and supplies of the traders needed to match identically.

(b) *A store of value*:   As money is durable it can be kept until the holder wishes to spend it. This ability to postpone consumption and thereby save facilitates better planning by individuals. Often, a rate of interest is offered by borrowers to attract lenders. Inflation reduces the real value of savings and necessitates an interest payment in order to attract people to store their money.

A rate of interest is determined by several factors such as risk involved, profit motive, market control, rate of inflation.

(c) *A measure of value*:   Money acts as a unit of account which enables goods and services to be valued. This allows consumers to make rational purchasing decisions by comparing prices. When goods are bought on credit, money acts as a standard for deferred payments and encourages trade which might not otherwise occur.

5.4.2 *The demand and supply of money*

The demand for money

There are three general motives why people wish to hold money rather than assets:

(a) *Transactions motives*: Money held ready to purchase goods and services, by cash or cheque. This demand is usually related to a person's *income*. For instance, people on high incomes have a larger transactions demand for money than those on state benefits. This demand may be manipulated slightly by government changes in benefits and tax rates. The *price level* may also influence the demand for money. At times of inflation, more money will be held because more is needed to buy the same amount of goods and services. The *frequency of payment* also affects demand. Transactions demand tends to be greater after a wage payment than before it.

An expectation of inflation will have the same effect.

(b)   *Precautionary motives*:   Most people keep some money available in order to meet unforeseen contingencies. The *real value* of such money is probably *lower* today than in the past, because the safety net of the state's *welfare* provision and *private insurance* minimize the financial costs of such emergencies. However, when *inflation* is rising people tend to save more in order to maintain the real value of their savings.

(c)   *Speculative motives*:   Some people hold money in readiness for a gamble. Such capitalist speculation was classically involving bonds but today there is a range of such assets. *Financial assets* range from low-risk and low-return savings certificates through to high-risk and (possibly) high-profit shares. Since 1979 share buying by ordinary individuals has risen substantially. In contrast, for most people, the purchase of *physical* assets, such as property, offers less quick rewards, although there may be a capital gain over time if the asset appreciates. Furthermore, physical assets are much more *illiquid* than financial assets and they are seen as necessary buys, in the case of houses. At times of high inflation, the speculative demand for money is likely to be relatively low. This is because the money held ready for speculation is losing its value quickly and so speculators will prefer its use in a revenue-earning asset. Generally it is to be expected that the rich will have a higher speculative demand than the poor. The overall demand for money is the *liquidity preference* curve. In order to encourage people to forsake money, interest is offered when they lend it or place money in a financial institution.

Privatization of the public sector, with underpriced shares and various incentive schemes for employees and consumers has encouraged share purchasing.

Some physical assets depreciate e.g. caravans and these tend to be those bought for leisure purposes.

Speculative demand is likely to be a residual amount, after transactions and precautionary motives have been fulfilled.

People demand money for the liquidity it gives them.

The supply of money

The supply of money is largely determined by the lending policies of the major clearing banks under the benign guidance of the Bank of England. However, measurement of the supply of money available depends on the *statistical definition* which is used. The '*broad*' measure of money used since 1976 has been sterling *M3* which is composed of coins, notes, private sector current and deposits accounts. In contrast, a '*narrow*' measure, *M1*, which excluded deposit accounts was about half the total value of M3. The narrowest measure, M0, adopted in 1982 to complement M3 contains just notes, coins and banks' balances at the Bank of England. The different measures tend to move in the same direction *but* the one adopted as the government's key target becomes the most unpredictable and variable.

This is clearly an academic discussion because to most people money includes building society deposits, which do not feature in these three definitions. The widest definition now called M5 does include them and some other private sector holdings of money market assets. M5 is about 50 per cent larger than sterling M3.

If we use a broad measure of money it is clear that the bulk of the money supply is concentrated in bank accounts, particularly current accounts. These can be created by the banks. They can give credit because not all cash deposits are quickly withdrawn. Also, some of the money lent to borrowers will be redeposited at the bank, thereby providing more cash reserves. An increase in cash may cause a multiple creation of credit. The money multiplier $=1/$cash ratio.

Remember 'Goodhart's Law' that once a monetary measure is chosen as a target it becomes distorted because the banking sector seeks to circumvent it.

A cash ratio of 10 per cent gives a money multiplier of 10.

A bank's ability to create credit is limited in theory by:

(a)   *Its cash ratio*:   The lower the cash ratio which it needs, the greater the amount of credit which can be created.

Don't forget there are many rates of interest.

At a high rate of interest there will be a low speculative demand for money, as the speculator will put his money in an interest bearing asset.

Liquidity trap – changes in money supply have no effect on interest rates

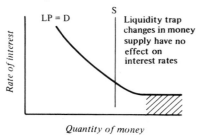

Quantity of money

Quantity of money

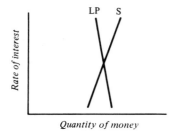

Quantity of money

Mainly for transactions motives, although borrowing to finance the purchase of privatized shares could be classified as speculation.

More capital only bought if interest rate falls so MRP curve (= demand) is normal shape.

This happens because at higher rates of interest, more people will forgo current consumption and lend money, thereby earning interest to enable greater future consumption.

Britain was in the early stages of stratoinflation between 1975–82; but hyperinflation, although common in Latin America, has never threatened in Britain.

(b)   *The Bank of England's behaviour*:   It could sell bonds and commercial bills in order to reduce the bank's cash base.

(c)   *The actions of other clearing banks*:   If they have higher cash ratios than the bank above, then this bank will face increasing indebtedness at clearing and its cash base will be lowered.

(d)   *The policies of other financial intermediaries*:   If they transfer funds out of a bank then its cash base will fall.

The price of money equals the rate of interest

The relationship between the demand for money and the rate of interest varies in different schools of thought. *Keynesians* made transactions and precautions demand interest inelastic but speculative demand was considered to be interest elastic. This analysis was based on *bonds* as the asset for speculation. The resulting liquidity preference curve was conventionally shaped and positioned, with the money supply being fixed by the monetary authorities.

For the *monetarists*, the demand for money was fairly stable, being mainly determined by transactions motives. They argued that an increase in money supply would lead to people holding larger money balances, ready for consumption. The money supply was again inelastic, but interest rates were more volatile than in the Keynesian model.

A more realistic approach is that the supply of money is not fixed but susceptible to the clearing banks' manipulation. They may expand the supply in order to earn higher profits. Furthermore the banks may influence the demand for money by their easily available credit schemes and persuasive advertising. There seems to be a high and *growing demand for money* as living standards improve, aspirations are raised and the opportunities for borrowing are increased. The fact that high real and nominal rates of interest have not choked off this demand infers its *inelasticity*.

Another theory was the *loanable funds* theory in which the rate of interest was determined by the demand for loanable funds and the supply of loanable funds. The demand was for money to purchase *capital* assets and was related to the marginal revenue product of the capital asset. As in the modern approach suggested above the supply of funds varied directly with the rate of interest.

5.4.3   Inflation

Since 1984, inflation has become less of a problem in the British economy. The annual rate has fallen and remained below 6 per cent. Thus the value of money has been less easily eroded, than in the late 1970s. Britain has returned to a *creeping* inflation without the fear of *strato-* and *hyperinflation*. Similarly, *stagflation* has abated as inflation has lowered, even though high levels of unemployment remain.

There are two main simple *causes* of inflation:

(a)   *Demand pull*:   This occurs when increases in demand pull up prices while supply is constrained. This may result from inadequate capital, a lack of trained manpower or a shortage of industrial space in specific firms or industries or the whole economy. The stimulants to demand may be fiscal or monetary. Tax reductions might increase spending power, as might cheaper and more readily available credit. By simple demand and supply analysis, this will cause higher market prices. Another possible boost for money demand arises from a balance-of-payments surplus.

(b) *Cost push*: This arises when costs increase unilaterally and prices go up as a result. The causes may be wage rises in excess of productivity improvements and higher-priced imported raw materials.

Keynesians and monetarists are divided over whether the impetus comes from an increase in the demand for money (which the extra supply of money accommodates) or from an increase in the supply of money (which causes more demand for money).

These two causes may be interrelated. For instance, a monetary expansion may stimulate demand; but, by facilitating company borrowing, it may also weaken their resolve in the face of wage demands thereby allowing cost pressures to push up prices. Purists maintain that the contributions of demand pull and cost push to inflation can be separated.

In a modern economy producers have the power often to pass cost increases on in the form of higher prices.

Higher profits may also be a cause of cost push inflation in some theories.

The *effects* of inflation are usually seen to be largely detrimental. People on *fixed incomes* become relatively worse off, as do those in weak bargaining positions and those in the public sector. Wage bargainers may press for increasingly higher *claims* each year to compensate for previous settlements which underestimated the rate of inflation. This could cause a wage-price spiral. Wealth is also *redistributed* usually to borrowers, who are paying a negative real rate of interest, from lenders; and to debtors from creditors.

A low rate of inflation is thought to benefit an economy, because it encourages business investment and production.

A negative real rate of interest means that the rate of inflation exceeds the rate of interest.

Consumer and producer behaviour may be harmed by inflation. Consumers may bring forward purchases or hoard, thereby *destabilizing markets*. Businesses may also suffer because planning and predictions become distorted and accelerating inflation *deters investment* and undermines business confidence. The consequences of such effects may be external in that a nation's *competitive position* can be undermined if its inflation rate exceeds those of its rivals.

Assuming exchange rate stability.

The *control* of inflation has been a policy objective of many governments. The approach tried varies with the perception of the underlying causes. The British Conservative government (1979–) adopted monetarist ideas, whereas earlier post-war governments, both Labour and Conservative, tried Keynesian remedies.

To monetarists the only cause of inflation is the excessive growth of the *money supply*. A surfeit of money activates demand pull. It also facilitates cost push because producers can finance cost increases, particularly wage rises, and then charge higher prices. Thus a growth in money supply leads to inflation after an eighteen-month time lag. The remedy is to slow down the growth of the money supply in the economy. Despite the adoption of monetary growth targets since 1979, it cannot be said that the supply of money had been successfully controlled. Some critics claimed that the 'wrong' monetary measures were targeted. Significantly, since 1982, there has been a search for other measures (M1, PSL2, M0) than M3, which was finally abandoned in 1986.

The rational expectations hypothesis is also relevant here in changing people's attitudes to future inflation.

More fundamental opponents of this monetarist approach argue that demand has been curtailed by a different method — old-fashioned *deflation*. Consumption and production was lowered by *high interest rates*,

Less need for output if stocks are run down.

A rising pound makes imports cheaper.

Also on-stream North Sea oil made the pound attractive to international financiers.

Higher taxes, lower government spending equals fiscal. Less credit, higher interest rates equals monetary.

Various experiments in the 1970s had a short-term dampening effect.

A facet of Conservative policy since 1981 has been to improve the training of school leavers but the approach used (YOP, YTS) has engendered a lot of scepticism.

Many attempts since 1979 to reduce trade union power because of its impact on costs via high wage claims, restrictive practices and overmanning.

Barclays, Lloyds, Midland, Nat West, Coutts, Williams & Glyns, the Co-op bank and Trustee Savings Bank.

1985 White Paper on banking reform intends to abolish the distinction between banks and licensed deposit takers.

'Deposit' sometimes called 'time' accounts. 'Current' sometimes called 'sight' accounts.

Direct debit, standing order, credit transfer.

which deterred borrowing and encouraged destocking. This lowered employment, thereby weakening trade union bargaining power and reducing wage cost increases. In addition, the propensity to import cost inflation was reduced because high interest rates kept the value of the exchange rate excessively high.

Keynesians, in contrast to monetarists, believe that the key cause of inflation is the *demand for money*. They believe that the supply of money is increased to accommodate demand requirements. In the short term, demand could be limited by *fiscal* and *monetary* restraints. Another policy option was *incomes policy* which sought to contain the wage cost element in inflation, thus inhibiting cost push elements.

However, the long-term solution was expansion of the productive capacity of the nation, so that increases in demand for goods/services could be met. Higher *productivity* and lower unemployment would raise supply so that monetary expansion would not be inflationary. The ability of a government to achieve productivity improvements is very limited, because deep-seated factors such as attitude, class, education and training are integral to the problem. All governments pay lip service to the need for better and more *investment*, but, outside the public sector, their capacity to influence events in a democracy is fairly low. The Keynesian emphasis on controlling the demand for money, whilst the supply side of the economy is restructured, implies government direction at a general level. In contrast, monetarists believe in less government involvement in society, although money supply needs surveillance and market imperfections require removal.

5.4.4   *The banking system*

Since the 1979 Banking Act a distinction has been made between '*recognized banks*' and '*licensed deposit takers*'. The élite amongst the recognized banks are the *clearing banks*. These *retail* banks take deposits from the public and lend money, via credit creation. In contrast licensed deposit takers are not allowed to create credit.

The clearing (commercial) banks perform four main functions:

(a)   *Accepting customers' deposits and safeguarding them in current and deposit accounts*:   Recently interest-bearing current accounts have been established for large depositors, so that the distinction between current and deposit is less obvious.

(b)   *Lending money*:   The credit card, loan and overdraft facilities earn substantial profits for the banks' shareholders.

(c)   *Transferring money*:   The banks move cash between branches, operate cheque-clearing facilities and provide various transfer services so that money is accessible and debts are honoured.

(d)   *Providing ancillary services*:   Modern banks have expanded the range of complementary services so that domestic and foreign commerce and trade can operate smoothly. Thus, cash dispensers, night safes, advice, foreign exchange etc., are provided to suit specific customer needs.

The monetary sector of the economy includes many other *financial intermediaries*. Many perform specialist functions within the capital and money markets. *Merchant banks* act as brokers bringing together the lenders and borrowers of large sums. They operate in high risks, give financial advice, negotiate bills of exchange, and underwrite new share issues. Such banks, like Rothschilds, are the *wholesalers* of money. *Overseas banks* have proliferated in London and most concentrate on dealing in foreign exchange. There are several government-sponsored banks, notably the *savings banks* and the *National Girobank*, which act as retail banks for small savers.

A unique feature of the British system is the *discount house*. The nine discount houses operate in the money market by borrowing for a short period from the clearing banks and lending for longer periods to other financial institutions. They have also diversified into money-broking.

Money broking refers to the movement of bank deposits and foreign exchange between financial institutions.

Financial intermediation is also performed by non-banking financial institutions. The most commonly known are the *building societies*. They differ from banks because of their friendly society status and non-profit-making aims. However, their services are increasingly similar and competition with the banks has intensified in the 1980s, aided by recent government legislation.

Competition through interest payments, credit cards, cheque books and home loans.

The main *institutional investors* do not compete with the banks. Organizations such as *pension funds* and *insurance companies* purchase securities and various other assets with the income which they receive from pension contributions and premiums respectively. The same function is also performed by *unit trusts* and *investment trusts* who speculate with people's savings.

Some of these traditionally distinct institutions have expanded and diversified. For instance, insurance companies have moved into unit trusts, home loans and estate agency.

5.4.5   *The Stock Exchange*

It is a market for the purchase and sale of *secondhand* securities. Since October 1986 the broking and jobbing functions have been merged and clients now deal with *market-makers*. Most of the transactions involve *company securities* but the highest value trade occurs in *gilt-edged stocks*. These are sold by tender. *Newly issued* shares are distributed by merchant banks, acting as issuing houses, with the authorization of the Stock Exchange Council.

Ordinary and preference shares.

Government and other public sector debt.

New issues may be by an offer for sale, by placing, by tender, by prospectus or by 'rights issue' (to existing shareholders).

The Stock Exchange provides an excellent example of a perfectly competitive market. There are many buyers and sellers with excellent knowledge and the ability to react rapidly to price changes. The demand for shares generally has increased significantly since 1979. The surge of '*people's capitalism*' is illustrated by the fact that 1.6 million people hold shares in British Telecom and there are estimated to be over 6 million individual shareholders in Britain. This growth has been fostered by *privatization*, government tax changes, improved living standards and better access to the stock market. In addition, a general mood of business optimism, faith in a government's monetary policy and political stability tend to make markets bullish.

Insider dealing uses a market imperfection (i.e. people with special knowledge) to make abnormal short-term profit.

1986 budget introduced the personal equity plan allowing a UK resident to invest up to £2,400 per annum with tax relief.

Several big city shops now provide share buying facilities.

The demand for specific shares is affected by many financial and economic factors. Demand is likely to rise if company *profits* rise, if company

In contrast, a bearish market means falling share prices.

profits exceed expectations, if a *takeover* is announced, and if rivals reveal higher-than-anticipated profits. Many of those demanding shares seek *capital growth* and so non-economic factors may carry more weight than a company's economic performance. This incites the criticism that the Stock Exchange enables rich speculators to bet on share price movements, rather than performing the more worthy tasks of directing funds towards *productive investment* and indicating those sectors of the economy with the best *business prospects*.

Critics of the Stock Exchange have also pointed to the weak supervision of companies and the unethical behaviour of some financial operators. The Financial Services Act 1986 was introduced to improve the protection given to investors from misleading and false statements by investment businesses and to illegalize insider trading. However, the current system of *self-regulation* through the Securities and Investment Board (SIB) does not seem to have been very effective e.g. Guinness scandal 1986–7.

There are several other small financial and quasi-financial markets in Britain. The *Unlisted Securities Market* (1980) enables trading in expanding companies which lack a stock market quotation. This is supervised by the Stock Exchange, whereas the *over-the-counter* market in smaller unquoted securities is administered by the National Association of Security Dealers and Investment Managers (NASDIM) under the general guidance of the Department of Trade and Industry. The *Lloyd's insurance* market handles many large commercial risks and its underwriters invest premiums in a diverse portfolio of financial assets. It is self-regulating too under the general supervision of the Department of Trade and Industry.

Some specialist agencies also provide finance. For instance, *Investors in Industry* (3i) provide loan and equity finance to companies. In the private sector, various *finance houses* and *leasing companies* provide instalment credit and rented capital equipment, thereby easing company cash flow.

International finance is a significant and developing feature of the British banking system. *Foreign exchange* is bought and sold at spot and forward prices. In addition, financial instruments, such as bills and bonds, are also traded via the *London International Financial Futures Exchange* (LIFFE).

5.4.6   The Bank of England

The central bank has two major responsibilities in the economy. It tries to ensure the *smooth running* of the banking system in order to maintain public confidence and faith in the stability of the system. More specifically it operates *monetary policy* on behalf of the government, in order to achieve certain objectives.

The Bank of England acts as the *banker's bank*. It keeps deposits of the banks and licensed deposit takers which are used in settling interbank debts. The Bank of England manages the national debt on behalf of the government and operates the *government's accounts*. It also holds the nation's gold and currency *reserves* in the Exchange Equalization account. These activities enable the system to function smoothly. It has the sole right of *note issue* and varies the distribution of notes and coins to meet seasonal needs.

In order to maintain confidence in the system, the Bank of England *supervises* the banks and other financial institutions. It sets certain 'prudential standards of liquidity to which banks should adhere'. The Bank of England will always provide cash to the discount houses when they have to repay loans and it will initiate rescue operations when a financial institution is in difficulties. The latter activity is known as the *lender of last resort*.

In addition to the passive and accommodating activities outlined above, the Bank of England has a more active and searching role in carrying out monetary policy. There are several *monetary controls* which can be utilized:

(a) *Assets ratios*: The Bank of England can vary, and has varied, these ratios in order to control the activities of the banks. For instance, if the objective was to limit the ability of the banks to create credit, the Bank of England could act to lower the banks' reserve assets ratio. This would give the banks a lower base to their *credit pyramid*. Over the years, the banks have thwarted such action, because it lowers their profit potential, by maintaining more than the ratio limit. The Bank of England has also partly undermined the effectiveness of asset ratio control by lending to discount houses so that they can pay back the banks who seek money at call repayment in order to restore their assets ratio.

(b) *Open market operations*:   The Bank of England can buy or sell bills and bonds in the money market, with the intention of affecting the banks' assets. For example, to restrict the banks' ability to create credit, the Bank of England will sell *bills* so that the buyers' cheques will be drawn on the banks, causing their balances at the Bank of England to fall. This lowers the cash base and limits the banks' credit-creating capacity. The sale of *bonds* is preferable to the Bank of England because the banks acquire an illiquid asset. Overfunding keeps the banks short of liquidity and interest rates high. This makes credit less available and more expensive. Generally, the Bank of England prefers sales of bonds and bills to the *non-bank private sector* rather than to the banks, because the former deprives the banks of assets. However, if the *government spends* the money from the sales of bills and bonds, then cash may be redeposited in the banks thereby replenishing their cash reserves and restoring their credit-creating potential. Despite open market operations, the banks can restore their cash base by reclaiming 'money at call' and forcing the discount houses to borrow from the Bank of England. However, this raises *interest rates* and could make borrowing more expensive, again possibly curtailing the demand for credit. Ironically, higher interest causes more borrowing in the short run because overdrafts become larger with the added (higher) interest charges. After a six-month time lag, the higher interest is effective in reducing the demand and supply of credit.

For instance, eligible banks must keep at least 2½ per cent of their eligible liabilities in money at call with the discount houses.

Johnson Matthey Bankers 1985.

Since 1945, banks have been given, at various times, cash, liquid assets and reserve assets ratios.

The prescribed ratio of acceptable assets is rarely changed because of the instability it would cause. For instance, from 1971–81 there was a 12½ per cent reserve assets ratio.

The Bank of England is acting as lender of last resort. However, by lending money to the discount market it charges a penal rate of interest and thereby raises interest rates, which it may not want to occur.

Overfunding means that the Bank of England sells more bonds than necessary, so depriving the banks of liquid assets (or cash) from which credit can be created.

The banks in acquiring bills (rather than bonds which are less liquid) obtain a fairly liquid asset, which could enable them to create credit thereby nullifying the open market operation.

For reasons of debt management, the government sometimes does not want higher interest rates, and so acts to undermine its own open market operations.

The idea was that the banks would restore their cash/liquid assets ratios by reducing their loans and thus credit would be restrained.

As these might impair the efficiency and profitability of the banks, they have not been used since 1979 – Conservative Party market philosophy.

Higher interest rates in 1980–1 pushed firms into destocking and raised the exchange value of the pound thereby making British exports more expensive and inflation lower.

The banks got around the supplementary special deposits scheme by disintermediation. This was where the banks rearranged some of the lending so that credit was created in ways not clearly seen in the accounts, to the chagrin of the Bank of England.

The credit boom in 1986 was largely stimulated by high street stores, such as Marks & Spencer, offering in-house credit cards.

Goodhart's Law implies the accuracy of monetary statistics is dubious, because the banks seek to circumvent Bank of England objectives if they are incompatible with profit making.

It assumed inflation was caused by excessive increases in money supply.

A transfer of funds from lenders to the government.

Although the sales cause the banks' balances at the Bank of England to fall, the subsequent government spending increases deposits and restores the banks' liquid assets.

(c) *Special deposits*:   These are a request that the clearing banks place some cash at the Bank of England, where it is frozen. They were introduced in 1960, and used up to 1980, in order to make open market operations effective. A quantitative control over deposits was introduced in 1973 (and disbanded in 1980). Banks had to remit supplementary special deposits to the Bank of England if their interest-bearing deposits grew faster than a specified rate.

(d) *Directives*:   These were instructions from the Bank of England to the banks. For instance, credit for exporters might be encouraged while lending for personal consumption might be deterred.

It is generally recognized that these monetary controls have not been very effective, particularly in curtailing credit creation, in practice. Interest rate changes seem to be marginally more effective than open market operations but they are often manipulated for other reasons such as the exchange rate. This may cause a *conflict of objectives*. Although higher interest rates may eventually curtail credit, they deter investment and possibly 'crowd out' the private sector, thereby inhibiting economic growth.

Another limitation on monetary policy is that the banks are in the *private sector* and often seek to nullify Bank of England initiatives in order to maintain their profitability. Furthermore, the ability of other financial intermediaries and retailers to create credit means that even if the Bank of England is successful with the banks, other agencies may undermine its monetary policy. The Bank of England is also reluctant to stifle the banks' *initiative* by overvigorous controls and this makes monetary 'control' weak. A further constraint on the Bank of England is that it makes decisions on out-of-date information, and economic estimates. This factor also undermines the effectiveness of monetary policy, which operates in an atmosphere of considerable uncertainty.

The general inadequacy of traditional monetary policy has led the government and Bank of England to turn towards *fiscal policy* in the pursuit of economic objectives. Since 1979 the Conservative government has tried to run a tight fiscal policy in order to lower inflation. Its medium-term financial strategy was concerned with the monetary effects of a public sector borrowing requirement. The effects of government *borrowing* vary with the buyers of the debt:

(a) *Non-marketable debt*:   Such as national savings, to individuals has no effect on money supply.

(b) *Bond sales*:   Bond sales to the non-bank private sector have no effect on money supply, but they could raise interest rates and thus reduce the demand for credit.

(c) *Bill sales*:   Bill sales to the banks raise the money supply, because the banks acquire a liquid reserve asset as well as extra deposits when the government spending occurs.

(d) *Borrowing from the Bank of England*:   This occurs when government securities are issued to pay for an increase in notes and coin in circulation. The latter arise at the banks' discretion and usually coincide with increased public demand for money. This effectively increases the money stock and raises the banks' potential for credit creation.

The recognition that the latter two methods of borrowing raise money supply has led to PSBR being financed mainly by the sales of bonds and non-marketable debt. In recent years the borrowing total from these two sources was overfunded so that it had a negative impact on the money supply statistics. It has also meant that the control of PSBR is an important objective of government policy. This is examined in Chapter 6.

Revision questions

1   Assess the effect of automation and microtechnology on employment.
(CIMA November 1986)

2   (a)   Why is the control of inflation considered to be important?

     (b)   What conditions would be necessary for inflation to be acceptable?
(CACA June 1986)

6
Macroeconomics

6.1 Topic relationship

This chapter builds on many of the concepts and ideas outlined in Chapter 5 on money and banking. It acts as a bridge between the individual market approach of several earlier chapters and the economic aggregates which are considered in Chapters 7 and 8.

The consideration of governmental economic decision making brings in most topics somewhere along the line. For instance, in examination of the yield from a tax, basic understanding of the operation of *demand* and *supply* is again required.

A modern discussion of public finance cannot be undertaken properly without reference to *monetary policy*. Similarly the fundamental differences between *monetarists* and *Keynesians* need to be understood before macroeconomic theories can be usefully discussed. Yet behind the discussion and policy initiatives, the basic desire to raise *national income* and thus *living standards* remains. This implies a concern for *poverty* and *wealth* distribution which has been less evident in most earlier chapters.

It is now largely accepted that changes in public finance affect monetary policy. For instance, increased government spending, ceteris paribus, means higher borrowing and thus possibly an increase in the supply of money.

6.2 Underlying concepts

A tax is a compulsory amount levied by the government or one of its agents (e.g. local authorities). The *formal incidence* of the tax falls on the person or institution charged with paying the sum over to the government. However, the *real incidence* may fall on someone else because the burden may be passed on via a price rise. The opposite of a tax is a *subsidy*.

Generally, the elasticity of demand for a good mainly determines how the burden is borne. Taxes on goods with relatively inelastic demand are more likely to be borne by the consumer, through higher prices, than by the producer, through lower profits.

Taxation in Britain is placed on *income* (e.g. corporation tax), *expenditure* (e.g. customs duties) and *capital* (e.g. capital gains tax). The amount raised in 1986–7 by each was as shown in Table 6.1.

A distinction is also usually made between *direct* and *indirect* taxation. With a direct tax, the person benefiting from the income pays the tax to the authorities e.g. income tax. In contrast, an indirect tax is remitted by the seller to the tax authorities but often charged to the consumer in the purchase price e.g. VAT.

Other taxes on income = national insurance, income tax. Other taxes on expendiutre = VAT, excise duties. Other taxes on capital = inheritance tax. There are many minor taxes placed on the use of assets, e.g. rates, motor vehicle licence duty, television licence fee.

The *marginal* and *average rates* of taxation, too, need differentiating. The average rate is the *total* tax paid as a percentage of total income; whereas the marginal rate is the *extra tax* paid as a percentage of an incremental rise in income. These different rates enable us to classify taxes into *progressive*, *regressive* and *proportional* categories. A progressive tax

For example, a person earns £10,000 per annum and pays £2,000 in tax, thus giving an average rate of 20 per cent. However, if his previous income was £9,000 and he paid £1,700 in taxation, his marginal rate of taxation for this income increase would be 30 per cent (i.e. $\frac{300}{1000} \times 100$ per cent).

has a rising marginal rate which is higher than the rising average rate. However, a regressive tax has a lower marginal rate with the average rate falling as income rises. The marginal and average rates are the same for proportional taxes.

The differing types and rates of tax enable assessment to be made about the merits of taxation. The principle of *equity* is usually considered to be necessary and the income tax system, which is progressive, is accepted as fair because the better off can, and do, bear a higher tax burden than the poor. Income tax is operated in a *certain* and *convenient* way, thereby illustrating two additionally important principles. The fourth principle enunciated by Adam Smith was *economy* i.e. cheap collection to maximize *tax yield*.

Two other (modern) principles have been suggested. Taxes need to be *efficient* in that they achieve their objectives and do not have deleterious side effects. Further, taxes should be *flexible* so that they can be adapted to meet new circumstances.

The revenues from taxation are used for public spending. This spending may be current or capital. *Current spending* is on goods and services used up immediately e.g. school books and VAT collection officers' salaries. However, *capital* spending involves the creation of assets e.g. schools, motorways which adds to the nation's wealth.

Public spending can also be differentiated in terms of the use of scarce resources. *Real* spending occurs when the public sector buys goods and services e.g. DHSS computers, and thus the finance is used productively. However, over 30 per cent of public spending consists of *transfer* spending whereby finance is redistributed from one group in society to another. For instance, much of the DHSS budget is used to provide income support through pensions and supplementary benefits, utilizing the money raised from taxpayers.

There are many uses to which public spending is put. '*Merit goods*' are provided at zero, or subsidized prices. These are services considered to be so desirable that the state provides them e.g. education for children aged five to sixteen. Also, the government creates '*public goods*' e.g. defence for the benefit of all society. These goods cannot be provided by the market because it is impossible to exclude non-payers from benefiting. Public spending is also used to *relieve* poverty, via transfer payments, and maintain *uneconomic goods* and *services* e.g. certain nationalized industries are financed from the public purse. Each nationalized industry has an *external*

Progressive taxes take an increasingly larger percentage of income in tax as income rises e.g. income tax.

VAT is a regressive tax and thus takes a higher percentage of the income of below average income families (compared to high income households).

The 'Robin Hood' principle is illustrated by progressive taxation.

People know what is expected and can easily (in an administrative sense) pay.

Tax yield is the amount accrued by the government.

For example, if an increase in income tax led to widescale evasion then it would not be efficient and its imposition could lower the government's tax yield.

When public spending is expanded less slowly than desired (perhaps for inflation control reasons), capital spending tends to be cut while current spending is maintained. This sacrifice is often made for political and administrative reasons.

Such spending does not add to national income because goods and/or services are not produced. In the national income accounts, this spending is deducted to prevent double counting.

The private sector may also provide 'merit goods' but they are sold at market prices e.g. private education.

A lighthouse is an excellent example of a public good because its service cannot be provided for one ship but not another.

Table 6.1

Income (£b)		Expenditure (£b)		Capital (£b)	
Income tax	41	VAT	22	Capital gains	1
Corporation		Excise		Capital transfer	1
tax	14	Petrol	7	transfer	1
National		Tobacco	4		
insurance	13	Alcohol	4		
		Customs	1		

These may be exceeded in exceptional circumstances e.g. British Coal (then NCB) 1984–5 because of the miners' strike.

These were introduced in 1976 for local government but now apply to over 60 per cent of central government spending.

financing limit designated to it by the Treasury. This is the annual maximum subsidy which it is allowed. The main government departments are given a similar spending constraint called *cash limits*. The DHSS is not limited in this way because its spending is *cyclical* i.e. changes in the economic cycle affect its spending. For instance, a depression raising unemployment will increase its departmental spending.

The balance between government income and spending and the effects of changes in the balance on the economy are the concern of *budgetary policy*. This term includes the old phrase 'fiscal policy' which mainly referred to management of the economy through changes in taxation. It also covers consideration of three closely related ideas — budget deficit, public sector borrowing requirement and public sector financial deficit:

The public sector is wider than the central government because the public sector also includes local authorities and nationalized industries.

- *Budget deficit* = central government income − central government expenditure
- *PSBR* = public sector current income − public sector current expenditure
- *PSFD* = public sector current + capital income = public sector current + capital expenditure

This is the most informative and less erratic measure of the balance because it shows the extent to which the public sector has acquired or lost financial assets. However, it is less popular with the government because it is calculated on an accrued, rather than actual cash, basis.

The PSBR is the official measure of the budgetary balance. Changes from year to year in the size of PSBR reflect the government's *fiscal stance*, with a higher PSBR signifying a more relaxed stance. A budget deficit increases the size of the *national debt*. This is the stock of all unpaid accumulated borrowing by the central government. The interest on the debt forms a significant part of public spending each year.

6.3 Points of perspective

Government macroeconomic policy is concerned with objectives such as inflation, unemployment, economic growth and the balance of payments. Intervention occurs because the operation of the market does not achieve the optimum allocation of resources or because it achieves a politically (and maybe socially) undesirable allocation of resources. Politics and economics are very difficult to disentangle and thus sometimes the government's economic policy oscillates between the political parties in power.

The 1979 Budget decision to lower income tax and raise VAT demonstrated the Conservative Party emphasis on individual freedom; and possibly their desire for a more unequal distribution of income to encourage initiative and enterprise.

It must be remembered that the Conservatives are not homogeneous, and the 'wet wing' is sceptical about monetarism and sympathetic to Keynesianism.

The Democrats and SDP tend to be 'conservative Keynesians'. They are critical of monetarism but less pro-Keynesian than Labour. For instance, at times of high unemployment they would increase PSBR but nowhere near as much as Labour would.

In recent times the two major British political parties have become associated with two contrasting *schools* of *economic thought*. The Conservatives have been linked with *monetarism*, which believes that inflation is the main cause of economic failure and that it can be controlled through regulation of the money supply. More generally, the monetarists believe that fine tuning of demand in the economy is pointless and that the *market mechanism* should be left to operate in an unrestrained way because it is inherently stable and efficient. Monetarists argued that fiscal management was irrelevant and that fiscal policy should be subservient to monetary policy.

The Labour Party has been associated with *Keynesianism*. Keynesian fiscal policy was explicitly adopted in the 1944 budget and pursued until the late 1970s, in order to stabilize aggregate demand by compensating for cyclical fluctuations in the market economy. Thus, government intervention was needed to rectify the failures of the market economy. Keynesians believed that fiscal policy was more effective than discretionary monetary policy, whose main objective was to manage the national debt and protect the exchange rate via interest rate manipulations.

In addition to these two schools of thought, there have been two other broad approaches. Towards the extreme right of the political spectrum, the *new classicals* have appeared. They advocated microeconomic policies to reduce *supply side rigidities* and stressed the importance of *rational expectations* amidst decision making. This approach was anti both fiscal and monetary policy.

Towards the left pole of the spectrum, some proponents of the *siege economy* briefly held court in late 1970s. They argued for British isolation, behind trade barriers and outside the EEC, so that the government could regenerate the British economy. This group of *new Keynesians* sought government *direction* through incomes policy and import controls rather than the traditional fiscal policy. Their fiscal policy would be targeted more towards the balance of payments than to domestic problems; and again they would place little emphasis on monetary policy.

The monetarist approach to economic management was tried in Britain from 1980 but largely abandoned in 1986–7. Interestingly, the Reagan government adopted monetarism 1980–2 but then instituted a traditional Keynesian fiscal approach to regenerate output and employment. The term 'Reaganomics' has been applied to the resulting 'loose budget' and 'tight money' policies aimed at lowering unemployment and containing inflation.

In judging the success of an economy often four macroeconomic objectives are taken into consideration — inflation, unemployment, economic growth and the balance of payments. The *Economist* devised a simple paradigm which gave a diamond shape for an economy. Figure 6.1 shows

The differences between monetarism and Keynesianism are considered in much more detail in Chapter 7.

The features of uncompetitive markets would need to be removed or reformed e.g. trade union power to make labour supply relatively inelastic.

For instance, if workers and employers quickly realize their mistakes and believe the government's economic pronouncements, then they will instantly modify their behaviour so that what the government wants is actually achieved.

The new Keynesian school is associated with the Cambridge Economic Policy Group.

Medium term financial strategy.

You should try plotting Britains's diamond with the current statistics. You will probably notice that the diamond is not symmetrical, and this shows the relatively weak part of the economy's performance.

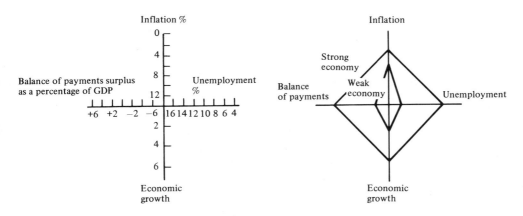

Figure 6.1 *The 'diamond' paradigm of economic performance*

the construction of the diamond and reveals that the bigger the diamond, the better the economy. If one part of the diamond is smaller than the other quarters, this demonstrates where remedial economic action could be taken by the government to rectify the weakness.

6.4   Essential knowledge

6.4.1   *Functions of taxation*

There are many possible aims of taxation and the priority which they are given might vary with the political party in government:

(a)   *Raise revenue*:   90 per cent of public spending is financed by taxation revenue with the remainder coming from asset sales, nationalized industry surpluses and borrowing. The relative importance of each type of taxation revenue varies between the political parties, with Labour tending to favour direct taxation in contrast to the Conservatives' liking for indirect taxation.

Between 1979–87 these asset sales included shares in public enterprises e.g. British Telecom, council houses and publicly owned land.

(b)   *Provide public goods and merit goods*:   These goods are produced by the state, which usurps the marketplace; no price is charged when they are provided because the necessary income comes from taxation. Generally, the Labour Party would prefer more widescale state provision, particularly of merit goods whilst the Conservatives would trust more to the efficiency of the free market.

The deregulation aspect of privatization and the withdrawal (or reduction) of public subsidies since 1983 illustrate the Conservative approach in this area e.g. bus transport.

(c)   *Change market behaviour*:   At a micro level, taxes often affect consumption e.g. a tax on cigarettes will raise price and probably reduce the quantity demanded. This reduction in consumption might be accompanied by a switch in expenditure to another product. However, customs and excise duties have tended to be used for the purposes of revenue raising in Britain, by both major parties, rather than for deterring the consumption of demerit goods.

(d)   *Manage the economy*:   Taxation is used to regulate economic activity. The Labour Party, which supports a Keynesian approach, would use fiscal policy to even out wild fluctuations in output, employment and prices. The Conservatives argue generally for lower levels of taxation and, if possible, a balanced budget. However, for them fiscal policy is subservient to monetary policy and therefore only indirectly influential over macroeconomic aggregates. Progressive taxation and unemployment benefit payments act as *automatic stabilizers* in an economy, and reduce the extremes of the business cycle. For instance, in a depression the existence of benefits prevents a massive fall in the income of the unemployed and thereby reduces the impact of the decline in consumption spending. Conversely, in a boom progressive taxation slows down the rise in net disposable income and perhaps reduces the growth of demand thereby limiting the inflationary pressure.

This could be done by running a higher PSBR (budget deficit) to reflate a slumped economy. For instance, lower taxation would stimulate spending, increase demand and lower unemployment probably.

(e)   *Alter the distribution of income and wealth*:   This function produces a marked difference between Labour and Conservative party policies. Labour believes in actively reducing income inequalities by levying progressive taxes. The Conservatives argue that such a policy destroys incentives and they prefer the tax burden to be more weighted onto indirect taxes, such as VAT. These taxes are usually regressive and thus their effect is to redistribute from poor to rich. Furthermore, Labour might introduce an annual *wealth tax*, in which the substantially better off pay a fairly small tax on the value of their assets beyond a threshold value.

Income tax is progressive, although since 1979 the top rate has been reduced from 83 per cent to 60 per cent.

In 1980 VAT was raised from 8 per cent to 15 per cent and its annual proceeds now exceed £41 billion.

6.4.2 Public spending

There are three main bodies which spend public money – central government, local government and nationalized industries. The largest proportion (three-quarters) is the expenditure of *central government* through its departments of state, which provide public goods, merit goods and transfer payments. *Local authorities* perform certain functions, such as education, at the discretion of, and with funds partially provided by, central government. The *nationalized industries* as a whole are largely self-financing, although individual public corporations may be dependent on public subsidies to cover their losses.

The rate support grant from central government to local government has fallen from 61 per cent in 1979–80 to 46 per cent in 1986–7.

The size and composition of public spending are significant economic and political issues. Through the 1970s and 1980s public expenditure has inexorably increased. This was partly accounted for by inflation. However, the ageing population, increased life expectancy and growth in unemployment have all contributed to rising spending. More has been expected of the *Welfare State* and so the growth in public spending has become *structural*.

For example, British Rail's total public subsidies exceed £750 million per annum.

However, even allowing for inflation, public spending in real terms has grown.

The exchequer cost in lost taxes (and national insurance) and paid out benefits exceeds £6,500 per person (1987).

The control of public spending has become a taxing problem for governments to face. Since 1976, the three main innovations have been:

(a) *Cash limits*: Each central government department and local authorities are given spending limits in cash bases on an inflation assumption for the financial year. Thus, if the volume of their spending or a negotiated pay bill exceeds assumptions, then cuts need to be made. Departments are not allowed supplementary estimates to finance overspending in the same cavalier fashion as in the early 1970s.

A 'structural' increase is one that occurs irrespective of economic trends. For example, public spending would increase in a boom as well as during a slump.

For instance, if public sector pay awards are expected to be 4 per cent and a deal of 6 per cent is agreed, then manpower will need to be cut or planned spending in some areas shelved.

(b) *Contingency reserve*: The total planned spending includes some unallocated expenditure. This can be used to meet unforeseen emergencies e.g. 1982 Falklands War. The reserve gives the Chancellor greater flexibility than in the past and enables forecasts to be closer to outturns.

(c) *External financing limits*: Each nationalized industry is given a target balance between its income and its expenditure. Profitable industries are expected to provide a surplus for the Treasury while loss makers are given subsidies.

Thus the Electricity Generating Board remits part of its £1 billion plus annual profit to the Treasury and this finances the loss making of (say) British Steel.

6.4.3   Public sector borrowing requirement

Measurement

A low PSBR purports to show a tight fiscal stance whilst a lower PSBR (than the previous year) indicates a tightening stance.

PSBR is the difference between two large accounting totals and it indicates the government's revenue shortfall which needs funding by borrowing. The annual PSBR figure shows the government's fiscal stance. The PSBR in Britain has followed a generally upward path since 1969, peaking at £13 billion in 1980. However, the 1987–8 outturn revealed a budget surplus again. The Conservative Party's medium-term financial strategy envisaged *PSBR falling absolutely and as a percentage of GDP.*

The 1987–8 PSBR was 1.25 per cent of GDP, compared with 5.5 per cent in 1978–9.

Table 6.2 Actual and demand-adjusted PSBR 1978–85

	Financial years 1978–9	1979–80	1980–81	1981–82	1982–83	1983–84	1984–85
Actual official PSBR (£b)	9.3	10.0	12.7	8.6	8.9	9.7	9.7
(% of GDP)	(5.4)	(4.8)	(5.4)	(3.3)	(3.1)	(3.2)	(3.0)
Public sector financial payments	−0.8	−1.7	−0.5	−2.0	0	1.9	1.8
Public sector deficit	8.5	8.3	12.2	6.6	8.9	11.6	11.5
Sales of land/ assets	0.1	0.4	0.8	1.7	2.3	2.1	2.0
Oil revenue	0.6	2.3	3.9	6.5	7.8	8.9	12.0
Demand- adjusted PSBR	9.2	11.0	16.9	14.8	19.0	22.6	22.5*
(% of GDP)	(5.3)	(5.3)	(7.2)	(5.7)	(6.6)	(7.5)	(7.0)*

*Cost of Miners' Strike = £36 deduction

A demand-adjusted PSBR shows the demand impulse on the economy in practice when the exceptional (one-off) items such as assets sales and oil revenues have been discounted.

The Economist calculated that the direct cost, via lost output and extra public spending on policing etc., of the miners' strike was £3 billion. However, others have argued that, after taking into account the indirect costs such as more expensive electricity and lost steel output, the economy suffered by at least £5 billion.

The era of high real interest rates (i.e. interest rate minus inflation) began in 1983.

PSBR is a nominal measure rather than a real (inflation adjusted) one.

A cyclically adjusted PSBR would indicate the size of PSBR needed given the state of the economy.

However, the annual targets were not consistently attained and the compilation of PSBR was criticized because dubious practices were used to lower PSBR. By use of the concept of a *demand adjusted PSBR* the *Economist* showed, in 1985, that the actual PSBR was much more relaxed fiscally than the Chancellor's public statements admitted. Table 6.2 shows that the oil revenues enabled a much lower PSBR than otherwise would have been the case and that a more accurate and sophisticated measure of the public sector behaviour indicated a large *demand stimulus* into the economy. Moreover, this demand impulse made the containment of money supply more difficult and probably necessitated higher than otherwise interest rates to dampen down consumer demand.

Another criticism of PSBR as a measure is that it does not adjust for *inflation*. Thus, a higher PSBR from one year to the next might reflect inflation rather than a more relaxed fiscal stance. Similarly, the idea of a *cyclically adjusted PSBR* has been suggested. Such a PSBR would be higher during a slump because higher unemployment necessitates greater spending on transfer payments and reduces tax receipts. Thus, a cut in PSBR when unemployment was rising would be a much tighter fiscal policy than a cut in PSBR when unemployment was falling.

Some critics of the Conservative government in the 1980s claimed that PSBR was too tight, given the economic climate. This was clearly a Keynesian view.

Effects

(a) *The Keynesian view*:   PSBR has *direct* fiscal effects on *output and employment*. For instance, a more relaxed fiscal stance (higher PSBR) is expansionary leading to increased consumer spending leading to greater production leading to greater employment. However, there may be *indirect* monetary effects on *interest rates*. The funding of public debt can be achieved by offering higher interest rates to attract lenders. This has a ripple effect on other interest rates and may deter consumption and investment. Nevertheless, Keynesians believe in using PSBR as part of a *discretionary* fiscal policy. They would use a larger PSBR, through tax cuts and public spending increases, to raise demand and lower unemployment. However, in the 1960s and 1970s such fine tuning activated a balance-of-payments crisis because of excessive consumption spending on imports. This provoked the reaction of deflation via a budget surplus (or smaller deficit).

More expensive borrowing inhibits consumption and makes some marginal investment projects unprofitable.

(b) *The monetarist view*:   A PSBR may cause *inflation* through its *indirect* effects on the supply of money. The effect depends on how the PSBR is financed. If the debt is sold to the *banks*, their assets are increased leading to a possible multiple expansion of credit. This increases the supply of money and causes inflation. However, if the loans are made to the government by the *private sector*, the effect on the money supply is largely neutral because funds are simply transferred between households (and financial intermediaries) on the one hand and the government on the other hand. It is possible that the government might *monetize* the debt. This occurs if the Bank of England issues notes and coins to pay for government borrowing. It gives the banks a bigger base to their credit pyramid and a greater likelihood that the money supply will increase. In practice, PSBR has been funded (and in some years overfunded) by sales of bonds and non-marketable debt. This has meant that public sector borrowing policy has not caused inflation. However, monetarists would argue that the option of borrowing from the non-bank private sector has depressed the economy through upward pressure on interest rates and the exchange rate. This indirect effect has resulted because higher interest rates are needed to sell government debt. As this leaves fewer funds for private sector investment it is claimed that the private sector is *crowded out* by the PSBR needs. The ideas of PSBR targets and the progressive reduction of PSBR were intended to control *inflation*. They also served as signals to the private sector that *markets* would become more orderly and stabilized. However, they probably intensified the increase in unemployment in the early 1980s.

The PSBR is financed by loans from different parts of the private sector i.e. households, financial intermediaries and banks. The main liabilities issued to these lenders are long-dated government stock (gilts), treasury bills and National Savings.

Bill sales give the banks a liquid asset (whereas bond sales provide a less liquid asset) which replaces the money spent, as well as the extra deposits when the government spending occurs. See Chapter 5.

The recognition that Treasury bill sales to the banks and the new issue of cash directly raise money supply have led the government to finance the PSBR from other sources.

Higher interest rates attract foreign funds to Britain and thereby increase the demand for sterling. This pulls the exchange rate up, thereby making British exports more expensive and potentially diminishing their share of world markets.

As monetarists believe in the primacy of the market this is anathema. It means that less efficient use is made of resources, when they are in the public sector.

6.4.4   *The national debt*

Marketable debt can be traded on the Stock Exchange.

Thus 92 per cent of the debt is owed to UK residents and institutions.

Index-linked stock receives an interest percentage above the rate of inflation (e.g. Treasury 2½ per cent 2024) which is also tax-free.

Much debt was accumulated to finance wars.

Capital investment would be a productive use e.g. motorway.

The monetarists would argue that these high interest rates would crowd out private sector investment and the extra borrowing would raise inflation. Together these would lower economic growth.

The monetarists claim that internal sales of debt crowd out private sector investment and distribute more resources to the public sector, which uses them less efficiently than the private sector.

This inflation meant that real interest rates were negative e.g. interest rate 15 per cent, inflation 18 per cent equals −3 per cent. However, in 1986 interest rate 10 per cent, inflation 4 per cent equals +6 per cent when real economic growth was 3 per cent.

Most of Britain's public debt is *marketable*, being composed of government stocks (70 per cent); of the remainder, about 20 per cent is non-marketable, mainly featuring National Savings Certificates. *Insurance companies and pension funds* together hold 40 per cent of the debt, while individuals and trusts account for 20 per cent and other financial institutions maintain about 15 per cent. Approximately 8 per cent of the £155 billion debt in 1988 was owed to overseas holders.

The *liquidity* of the national debt varies from three months to thirty years for dated stock, with some index-linked stock redeemable in the year 2024. Some government stock is also undated e.g. Consols 4 per cent. If the average debt length increases because more long-dated stock and fewer shorts are issued, this policy is termed *funding*.

The cost of debt *servicing* increases with the total size of the national debt. This servicing cost affects both the yearly budget and the economy in general:

(a) *Budgetary effects*:   The interest payments must be met either out of current income or by more borrowing. This involves an opportunity cost. Effectively, there is a transfer from taxpayers or public service recipients to holders of the debt. Moreover if previous debt was issued to finance current expenditure the debt would be a deadweight burden. However, if the original debt had been effectively used by the public sector, then the current population might be benefiting indirectly.

(b) *General economic effects*: The impact of the national debt's servicing depends on *how it is financed* and *by whom*. If the government borrows, then interest rates may rise, probably. In contrast, if the government raises taxes or cuts public spending then the economy may be depressed and unemployment might rise. Most debt is sold internally but *overseas sales* lead to a future drain on resources when interest payments are remitted abroad.

Budget deficits have become *structural*, thereby increasing total public debt each year. Mr Evsey Domar argued that these deficits were not a burden as long as *real economic growth* exceeded *real interest rates*. In the 1960s and 1970s the real burden of the national debt fell because inflation rose rapidly. National debt fell as a percentage of GDP, so the government gained as inflation exceeded interest rates and debtholders lost. However, since 1984 the faster fall in inflation has made the debt burdensome.

One way to pay the rising interest payments, and avoid tax rises (or spending cuts), without further borrowing, is to *monetize* the annual deficit. However, if the government prints money to fund PSBR then it risks future inflation, particularly in the monetarist analysis. Ironically, this might relieve the debt burden but if it changed people's expectations interest rates might also rise.

6.4.5   *Economic objectives*

Those with influence in an economic system usually seek to raise *living standards*. This vague general objective is supported by more specific aims:

(a) *A low level of inflation*:   In the 1980s 5 per cent or less was considered as acceptably 'low'.

(b) *Full employment*:   The objective in the late 1980s has become to reduce unemployment to less than 3 million.

Between 1945–79, unemployment rarely passed 1 million.

(c) *Balance-of-payments surplus*:   This objective is often not at the discretion of governments e.g. North Sea oil receipts giving Britain a surplus, despite a large deficit on manufacturing trade.

(d) *Significant economic growth*:   Britain's post-war growth average of 2.5 per cent is relatively poor, but it has been sufficient to raise the standard of living substantially. A national crisis, such as the miners' strike 1984–5, can slow down growth.

There is often some dispute between commentators over economic objectives and *intermediate targets*. For instance, a *stable exchange rate* might be seen by some as an objective whereas to others it is a target. As a target it enables the fulfilment of other objectives. For instance a steady exchange rate means that inflation is not imported via a depreciating pound, and trading patterns might be stabilized.

Targets are often short-term objectives e.g. in 1987, the Conservative government set targets for the pound sterling against the dollar ($1.60) and against the deutschemark (2.99dm).

Another possible economic objective is the *redistribution of income and wealth*. A Labour government would seek to reduce income inequalities in society, by various fiscal policies. However, this has not been an objective of Conservative governments although they support the Welfare State and the relief of poverty.

The Conservative record 1979–87 shows a widening of the gap between rich and poor both in income and in health.

As well as contention about the list of economic objectives, there is argument over the *priorities*. In so far as governments are able to assist in the pursuit of the objectives, the priorities vary over *time* and between political *parties*. For instance, from 1979 to 1986 the Conservative government's main objective was to lower inflation substantially but from 1986 it seemed to switch towards rectifying the unemployment crisis.

6.4.6   *Government policies*

There are many different policies which governments use in attempting to fulfil the main economic objectives. The most important are *monetary* and *budgetary* (fiscal) policy. The importance and emphasis placed on each varies with the political complexion of the government and the nature of the problems faced.

Monetary policy was detailed in Chapter 5 and budgetary policy was outlined earlier in this chapter.

Usually, the policies are/were used to affect the major *macroeconomic variables* in the economy – consumption, investment, output, employment, inflation, money supply, balance of payments, exchange rate. For instance, a tight monetary policy might lower consumption and lower investment causing reduced output and more unemployment. However, it could reduce inflation and aid the balance of payments, despite

The relationships between many of these variables are considered in Chapter 7.

Ironically, the Labour government 1974–9 developed an industrial policy of intervention, via the National Enterprise Board (and various development agencies) aimed at extending public ownership as well as propping up the ailing parts of British capitalism. Since 1979, many of the assets brought into public ownership in that period have been returned to the private sector via privatization.

Regional policy was examined in Chapter 2.

Competition policy was examined in Chapter 3.

Thus the Conservatives ended restrictive practices on the stock market to the chagrin of many of their traditional political supporters.

In particular, the closed shop has been weakened by the institution of regular reviews by secret ballot; and strike activity has been discouraged by the introduction of codes of practice for picketing and the necessity of strike ballots.

Youth Training Schemes, Technical and Vocational Education Initiatives, Training Opportunities Schemes, Industry Training Boards.

However, labour immobility occurs for other reasons i.e. personal and social.

From 1975 to 1977 Labour ran a two-stage legally backed incomes policy. In Stage 1, a £6/week maximum pay increase was allowed and in Stage 2 it was 5 per cent (or £2.50 to £4 maximum.) In the two years to 1979, the policy was voluntary with a 10 per cent guideline followed by a 5 per cent guideline.

This explanation suggested that the money supply controls were not working to quell inflation.

Thus a fall in raw material prices and a rise in the exchange rate would doubly benefit the British economy.

reducing aggregate demand in the economy. This was, in essence, a Keynesian approach.

The rise of monetarism has led to greater consideration by governments of *microeconomic decision making*. Thus, government interference in the structure and performance of various markets and industries has occurred. The generic term '*industrial policy*' has been developed to cover a myriad of initiatives in this realm. The 1972 Industry Act gave the government powers to provide selective assistance, in addition to the automatic, general assistance which *regional aid policies* offered. It is likely that a Labour government would seek close liaison with major British firms on an individual level in order to co-ordinate public and private sector economic activity.

Competition policy has been promoted as a strand of industrial policy. It seeks to improve the efficiency of markets by the control of monopolies, restrictive practices and nationalized industries; and to encourage competition by privatization and help to small firms. To monetarists, the furtherance of competition also applies to labour markets. This has meant, since 1980, a reduction in *trade union* power by legislation and an increase in *training* provision by various schemes. The Manpower Services Commission was expanded enormously with the intention of producing a higher-quality workforce. Its work supplements the skill centres which train redundant workers in new skills. The general aim was/is to make labour more mobile, thereby generating more efficient labour markets.

The problem of inflation has produced two distinctive policy responses. The 'old' policy tried mainly in the 1970s was *incomes policy*. This was direct action by the government to limit wage, and sometimes price, increases for a short period. It attempted to lower the cost push element in inflation and might be labelled a Keynesian approach.

The 'new' policy used in the 1980s was the *exchange rate*. If the exchange rate appreciated, this acted to make imports cheaper and thereby undermined inflation. Some economists argued that the massive rise in sterling's value, prompted by North Sea oil, was largely responsible for the fall in inflation in the early 1980s. Beckermann claimed that falling commodity prices were also a major contribution to lower inflation in many economies. Significantly, after the pound plummeted to $1.06 in 1986, the British government maintained its relatively high interest rates in order to keep the pound up. In 1987 the Chancellor formally admitted that the government had an exchange rate target, and thus an exchange rate policy.

6.4.7 *Policy constraints*

The intentions of an economic policy and its results are rarely, if ever, exactly the same and sometimes diverge. This happens because of the limitations faced by governments when policy making. Problems occur during policy formation and operation.

The main constraints on policy making are:

(a) *Information*:   A plentiful quantity exists but it is of variable quality. Government statistics are often *out-dated* because of the time needed for collection and based on *estimates* because of the difficulty of collection. Thus the information, upon which decisions are made, is less than perfect.

(b) *Understanding*:   The knowledge of *how* the economy operates is imprecise. The interrelationships between variables are not fully understood; and different groups of economists have different *explanations* for the same changes. Their *assumptions* about the operation of the economy vary and thus so do their predictions of the effects of policy initiatives. Thus, there are many economic models based on complicated *equations*. The models of the different economic forecasters tend to make predictions in the same direction but at different speeds with varying side effects.

(c) *Timing*:   It is possible that the government's review of a current position may be inaccurate and so a policy initiative may be addressing the wrong problem. Furthermore, many policies take months to become operational and effective, by which time the problem may have disappeared or changed. For these, and philosophical reasons, monetarists argue that the *fine tuning* of the economy, most associated with Keynesianism, is possibly counter-productive and certainly dangerous.

(d) *Inefficiencies*:   Some methods are not as effective as their advocates believe. This means that success *expectations* may be unduly high. For instance, it was believed that incomes policy would curb inflation. This was achieved in the short run but when direct government intervention was ended inflation took off again. Moreover, a method may be inefficient in that it has destabilizing *side effects*. For instance, Keynesians would probably argue that a tight budgetary policy aimed at inflation will make unemployment worse and thereby weaken an economy. The various economic schools have differing *perceptions* of the efficiency of policy instruments. Keynesians rate budgetary policy as superior to monetary policy which the monetarists prefer. Monetarists generally are more pessimistic about the ability of any government policies to influence economic decision making.

(e) *Externalities*:   Destabilizing events, both at home and abroad, can wreck the intentions of a policy. These externalities may be both economic and political. Britain is very susceptible to external economic shocks because of its dependence on *trade* and its *open* economy. For instance, the oil price hike 1973 undermined the Conservative government's policy to combat inflation. The world depression in 1981 intensified the decline of British manufacturing industry.

Political requirements sometimes affect economic policy making. For instance, in 1987, public spending plans increased significantly thus enabling the government to defuse the opposition's claim that it was unconcerned about health, education and social services. A change of party in government may also cause the premature ending of one policy. This was illustrated by the (eventual) reversal in regional policy spending when the Conservatives took over from Labour in 1979.

For example balance of payments invisible account.

The Treasury model of the economy has over 700 equations whereas NIESR has only 100.

For instance, a £1·5 billion of public investment would raise GDP by 0.9 per cent in the NIESR model, but by only 0.5 per cent in the London Business School model. However, the NIESR model shows a 0.4 per cent increase in inflation as a result of the public investment whereas the LBS prediction is higher at 0.6 per cent.

Although changes in VAT can be made overnight, income tax changes usually take at least two months to come through.

The monetarist alternative is a series of 'policy rules' e.g. medium-term financial strategy.

Opposition parties suffer from 'hubris' and they have a greater optimism for their ability to manage the economy, better than their predecessors have done.

In 1983, a House of Commons Select Committee attributed the dramatic increase in unemployment equally between government anti-inflation policy and world trade factors.

It is often suggested that chancellors engineer pre-election consumer booms in order to influence public opinion, irrespective of the underlying economic needs. Economic growth in election years exceeds other years by 0.3 per cent on average.

Prior to 1979, regional aid expenditure had been rising, but the Conservatives steadied and then reduced such funding, after 1985.

6.4.8   Policies in the 1980s

Britain

The 1980 monetary targets for the percentage increase in £M3 were:

1980–1	*7–11 per cent*
1981–2	*6–10 per cent*
1982–3	*5–9 per cent*
1983–4	*4–8 per cent*

However, these were revised after the first year overshoot and by 1986 such targetry had been abandoned.

An even higher monetary policy might have deepened the depression undesirably, particularly through even higher interest rates.

Ironically, the commercial banks with their competitive instincts were a major stumbling block because they expanded credit (for profits) beyond the government's money supply targets. Direct control over the banking sector could have stopped this but it was counter to the Conservative government's market orientated politics.

See Section 3 above for discussion e.g. special asset sales, nationalized industries' borrowing.

Around 4 per cent.

Privatization occurred in three ways – sales of public sector assets, deregulation of certain services, and increased competitive tendering particularly of public services.

From 1980 to 1986 the Conservative government's policies centred around its *medium-term financial strategy*. This monetarist approach contained a series of targets for key economic variables, such as £M3 and PSBR, based on the premise that '*control of the money supply* will over a period of years reduce the rate of inflation'. However, hindsight has shown that monetary control is, and was, technically more difficult than most monetarists realize (realized). Several money supply measures were tried and given wide target bands, but with persistent failure the experiment was largely abandoned in 1986 with £M3's demise. It had become clear that the government lacked the will and the means to effectively control money supply growth. Nevertheless, inflation fell, arguably more because of deflation, the exchange rate and world commodity prices rather than because of money supply control.

The plans to reduce the *absolute* and *relative size of PSBR* were largely successfully fulfilled. The PSBR was directly under the government's control and so more amenable than money supply. However, critics have argued that PSBR is a poor economic indicator because the figures can be manipulated in several ways.

In 1987, the movement away from money supply targetry and the adoption of a PSBR rise in real terms were seen as the ending of MTFS. Chancellor Lawson's more pragmatic approach since 1984 had presaged this change. However, the government could argue that the aim of MTFS had been achieved, in that *inflation was brought under control*, and the conditions for *sustainable economic growth* had been created.

The prevailing philosophy of less government interference in economic decision making was illustrated in several other policy areas. Government funding of *regional aid* was cut in money and real terms, while *competition* was encouraged by *privatization*. In addition, the government tried to increase the *efficiency of markets*. Their competition policy was aimed at removing supply side rigidities. Ironically, in some cases, it required legislation (e.g. trade union laws) and intervention (e.g. government loan schemes and labour subsidies) to engender an enterprise culture.

America

Critics claimed that this was resurrected Keynesianism but the US Treasury argued that it was a supply side approach, with the lower marginal tax rates aimed at raising tax revenue through a Laffer curve effect from incentives.

USA suffered huge balance of payments deficits in the mid-1980s. In 1987, this prompted calls for protection, particularly against Japan, Third World textiles and EEC steel, as the dollar dramatically weakened.

While Thatcherite economics reigned in Britain, 'Reaganomics' operated in America. Initially the two were very similar in their approach to fiscal and monetary policy. However, from 1982, the American government went for a *loose budget* and *tight money*. It slackened fiscal policy with the intention of raising output and employment. Within three years 9 million new jobs had been created and real capital spending had risen by 20 per cent. The fall in inflation, ostensibly caused by the prevailing tight monetary policy, meant that real consumer spending had grown significantly.

Sceptics sought other explanations for this great improvement in living standards. The fall in inflation could be attributed to the strong dollar which kept imported prices down. Part of the economic boom was probably financed by external funds which were attracted by the high interest rates, while the big budget deficit stoked consumption spending in the traditional Keynesian way.

Supply side initiatives were also introduced in the USA. The Workfare Scheme has perhaps made the labour market more flexible, but it was more elastic than Britain's anyway because of the decentralized economy and federal structure.

Revision questions

1 (a)   What factors determine exchange rates?
   (b)   How do you account for the high price of the US dollar in relation
         to other currencies in 1984 and 1985?   (CACA June 1986)

2 Who will gain and who will lose if a country imposes restrictions on its
   imports in order to protect certain of its industries?
                                                    (CACA December 1985)

Workfare is a welfare system in which able-bodied recipients (such as long-term unemployed) are required to work or take special training/education in return for continued welfare payments.

Less welfare is granted to the unemployed in America and this makes the labour market more flexible probably. Also, wages are often fixed over 2–3 year contracts. NIESR suggested that this fact means that 'real wages' grow more slowly in USA.

7
Government and the economy

7.1 Topic relationship

The relationships between the major *economic aggregates* are central to this chapter. Within this context *general theories* are devised and related to the two broad *schools of economic thought* – Keynesian and monetarist.

See Points of perspective, Chapter 6.

Each government has certain *aims* and definite priorities for an economy. These objectives were outlined in Chapter 6 and illustrated in Figure 6.1. (See page 65.)

(a) A low level of inflation.
(b) Full employment.
(c) An equilibrium balance of payments.
(d) Satisfactory economic growth.
(e) A steady exchange rate.

A government has certain tools at its disposal to achieve these objectives. *Fiscal* and *monetary* policy are tools which are assigned roles in order to achieve these objectives. Each policy has *instruments* which can influence specific *intermediate targets* so that the objective becomes more possible.

For instance, in the 1980s monetary policy occupied a central position in macroeconomic management in the United Kingdom. Its objectives were to give economic stability and reduce inflation. The medium-term economic strategy co-ordinated the instruments designed to achieve these objectives. The main instruments were interest rates and PSBR and these acted on the intermediate target which was the rate of growth of the money stock. The strategy was to set target growth ranges for the money supply. These ranges would be reduced in succeeding years so that, in theory, inflationary pressures would be squeezed out of the economy.

Originally a single aggregate M3 was chosen as a target, but in 1982 M1 + PSL$_2$ were added because of the former's unreliability. In 1984 the authorities dropped PSL$_2$ and replaced M1 with M0. However, in 1987 M3 was also dropped.

The most recent published ranges were:

Time period	Money supply measure	Growth range Target	Actual
February 85	Sterling M3	5–9	14.8
– April 86	M0	3–7	3.5
February 86	Sterling M3	11–15	
– April 87	M0	2–6	
February 87	M0	2–6	
– April 88			

Other macroeconomic policies tend to be less significant, although *exchange rate* policy has become more noticeable in the 1980s. Its importance has grown for two reasons. First, a change in the exchange rate affects domestic prices and thus counter-inflation policy. Thus, an appreciating exchange rate keeps the price of imports slightly lower. Second, the exchange rate indicates monetary conditions. This happens because if international investors have confidence in the effectiveness of monetary policy it causes an exchange rate rise in advance of the policy's operation.

In contrast, *incomes policy* has become less discussed in the last decade. It was advocated by cost push theorists and implemented in the 1970s in order to control inflation. The underlying theme was that trade union pushfulness was an exogenously determined cause of inflation. Although the Conservative government since 1979 would concur with this view of trade union activity, their opposition to state intervention in market decision making has meant that incomes policy has not been utilized.

7.2   Underlying concepts

Economists and governments are concerned with the state of national income. An *equilibrium* level of national income is desired where full use of all resources obtains. It occurs where the planned actions of *economic agents* are fully realized. However, in practice all economies are in *disequilibrium* because planned and realized actions do not correspond. When this happens planned expenditure and planned output are not equal. If the latter exceeds the former then stocks may accumulate. Sometimes existing planned levels of stocks are run down because of unexpectedly high spending – this is known as *destocking*.

The main determinants of national income are *investment* and *consumption*. Together with *government spending* they compose aggregate monetary demand. In economic management, governments are concerned with such *aggregate measures*. In order to influence the economy, the government initiates policies which affect the *various sectors* i.e. household, firms, government, international.

As national income measures the value of national output produced, it follows that investment which influences output levels thereby affects the growth of national income. The amount of investment needed to produce a volume of output is called the capital-output ratio. Thus more and better-quality investment will tend to raise national income, *ceteris paribus*.

Similarly, more consumption spending by households will generally raise national income, although spending on imports is wasteful from a nationalistic point of view. Savings tend to detract from national income growth because they reduce consumption levels. However, in the long run, if the savings are translated into investment then they may be beneficial. *Dissavings*, whereby savings are used for consumption purposes, may give a once-and-for-all boost to an economy.

The idea that money flows between different sectors and for different purposes is central to national income determination. In this *circular* flow of income, equilibrium occurs if planned *injections* equal planned *leakages*. Injections which add to spending such as investment, export earnings and government spending tend to raise national income. In contrast, leakages which are withdrawals of potential spending such as savings, taxation and import spending, lower the growth potential of national income. If planned leakages exceed planned injections then consumer spending is less than anticipated and producers accumulate stocks. Subsequently, producers destock and so do not produce as much output, thereby reducing national income.

The exchange rate thus tends to be a 'leading' indicator, with its increase indicating that monetary policy will be compatible with a government's domestic economic objectives.

Critics have argued that public spending planning totals and cash limits were a veiled form of incomes policy adopted in the public sector.

These are explained later in the chapter.

For example, if £10,000 of investment enables £5,000 of goods to be produced in one year then the capital-output ratio is 2:1.

It must be remembered that national income = national output − national expenditure.

The velocity of circulation is the number of times over a period of time (usually one year) that each unit of currency is spent.

Interest rates are lower because the demand for money is interest rate inelastic i.e.

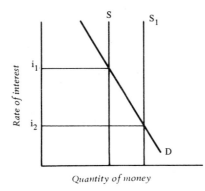

Quantity of money

To Keynesians, the demand for money is more interest elastic and so interest rates are less likely to fall. Also, the extra money may be held for speculation rather than consumption.

Keynesians believe that the supply of money is endogenous, being determined by the level of income in the economy.

This chain of causation shows that in a complex economic system a stimulus may have short and long-term effects, as well as a feedback influence. This makes effective economic management by a government incredibly difficult.

The government creates an environment in which consumer sovereignty prevails and producers flourish.

The way in which money flows throughout the economic system can be crucial. Keynesians and monetarists dispute over the *transmission mechanism*, which is the route which a change in money supply takes through the economy. The monetarists argue that the *velocity of circulation* is unaffected by changes in money supply. The result is that increased holdings of money will be spent on goods and services and lower interest rates will stimulate further spending. This, in turn, causes price rises and output increases.

Keynesians, in contrast, believe that changes in money supply have little impact on output. The velocity of circulation may change to nullify the impact of an increase in money supply. Also, the growth of money supply may not be translated into consumption and so need not necessarily cause inflation.

Such issues open up the general notion of determinism. In an economic system it is important for a government to know how variables are interrelated. If a variable is *exogenously* determined, it means that it is dependent upon an outside stimulus. For instance, monetarists believe that the supply of money is exogenous. However, most major economic variables are endogenous. Thus a change in one affects another. For example, an increase in national income raises consumption which may eventually further increase national income.

7.3   Points of perspective

Keynesians and monetarists disagree over two fundamentals – the market and real, as opposed to monetary, forces. Monetarists believe in the efficiency of the *free market*, claiming that prices stimulate risk taking and competition. This leads to the efficient allocation of resources and so the role of any government should be limited to that of a *nightwatchman*. The intervention, which Keynesians advocate, will be destabilizing and eventually harmful because unregulated markets automatically adjust and restore equilibrium. Keynesians argue that producer sovereignty has replaced consumer sovereignty and thus discretionary government intervention is necessary to stabilize individual markets and regulate the whole economy.

Monetarists make a distinction between *real and monetary forces*, which Keynesians discredit. The market forces of demand and supply cause real changes in output and relative prices but the supply of money determines the overall price level. In contrast, Keynesians claim that changes in the supply of money can produce real variations in output and employment.

One consequence of these differences is that Keynesians prefer *fiscal policy* as a policy instrument to achieve certain objectives. Monetarists, on the other hand, wish to protect markets from such governmental interference and so prescribe certain *policy rules* and a limited use of *monetary policy*.

Despite these two schools of thought, more economists are taking an *eclectic view*, and questioning parts of the respective theories. Also, there is agreement between Keynesians and monetarists in some areas, such as the determinants of the demand for money and the general belief that changes in money supply and the general price level are correlated.

In a similar view, it should be noted that governments have become less loyal to their school of economic thought. Since 1982 the Conservative government has become more pragmatic in its approach to targets and more reserved about their usefulness as indicators. As the Governor of the Bank of England said:

> Monetary targetry is only a means to an end. There may be circumstances in which the relationship between the intermediate target and the end objective changes unpredictably. . . . In that case if the marksman does not have the wit to adjust his aim he may inflict severe injury on the economy.

The Labour government 1974–9 adopted some monetarist notions from 1976 and effectively controlled money supply 1976–9. However, the Labour Party is more avowedly Keynesian than monetarist, and has blamed many of Britain's 1980s' problems on dogmatic adherence to monetarist ideas.

7.4   Essential knowledge

7.4.1   *Consumption*

The amount of consumption, both by individual households and by a whole economy, is determined by the level of *income*. In Keynesian theory $c = a + by$.

This happened in 1980s. See Goodhart's Law. Also market deregulation of the financial services sector and the resultant competition between banks, building societies and other financial intermediaries has meant the monetary authorities cannot be confident of the interrelationships anymore as they are evolving.

a = autonomous consumption, which does not vary with income.
b = marginal propensity to consume, which is related to income.
y = income.

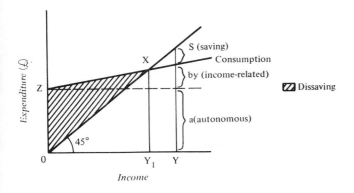

Figure 7.1   *The Keynesian consumption function*

The slope of the consumption curve indicates the *marginal propensity to consume*. If MPC fell, then the curve would be flatter. A fall in MPC causes a fall in the *average propensity to consume* (APC). In the British economy it is assumed that both MPC and APC fall as income rises but both are positive and exceed 0.7.

The factors determining consumption can be considered by sector. For *households* the main influences are:

(a) *Income*:   There are several theories related to this most important factor. Friedman has proposed that *permanent* income rather than temporary income determines the size of long-run MPC and APC. Keynes emphasized *present* income while others have proposed that *previous* income or *relative* income may be significant.

APC = proportion of disposable income which is consumed.

Households' and firms' consumption spending account for 60 per cent of domestic spending, whilst the government's share is 23 per cent. Investment spending contributes the other 17 per cent of the total.

In late 1986 and 1987 a consumer boom occurred in Britain because the banks and high street retailers extended their credit card activities.

(b) *Wealth*: For individuals, the acquisition of wealth by whatever means will probably raise APC because less saving will be needed and dissaving can be undertaken. For society generally a less unequal distribution of wealth will probably raise consumption.

(c) *Credit*: The cheaper the cost and the greater the availability of credit, the more likely it is that consumption will occur. Thus an increase in the rate of interest may deter consumption.

(d) *Government policy*: An increase in direct taxation reduces disposable income and lowers consumption, as does a rise in indirect taxation. Conversely, higher state benefits raise income and thereby generate more consumption.

Apart from these general influences, there are also *subjective factors* which affect specific individuals. For instance, people living in rural areas and those who are tightfisted tend to consume less than others of similar means.

The consumption by *firms* is determined by the above four factors. However, slightly different terms are used:

(a) *Sales revenue* which is a firm's income.

(b) *Accumulated reserves* which are its wealth.

(c) *Borrowings* which cover credit and capital.

(d) *Government policy*.

Higher government spending causes a higher level of income (rather than vice versa) because taxes can be raised to obtain the necessary revenue.

Consumption spending by the *government* is less dependent on its income because the income level is accommodated to fit the spending plans. These are determined by *political decisions* at Cabinet and Treasury level. Individual government departments, specific nationalized industries and local authorities have some discretion over their spending.

It must be noted that some government departments, such as DHSS, spend money in providing social security, which enables people to consume goods and services. This DHSS spending is an example of transfer payments while that of Ministry of Defence is classified as consumption.

7.4.2   Savings

The level of saving is determined by income mainly and usually represented by the equation $S = Y - C$. In Figure 7.1 saving is positive beyond X and negative between 0 and X. Negative saving is termed *dissaving*. In the British economy, the APC is 0.1. The savings ratio is composed of *contractual* and *discretionary* savings.

Contractual savings are generally stable and uninfluenced by changes in the economic cycle.

The discretionary savings of *households* are determined by:

(a) *Income*: As savings tend to be a residual after consumption has occurred, the factors influencing consumption thereby indirectly affect savings.

This is a substitution effect.

This is an income effect.

(b) *Interest rates*: If the rate of interest falls, people might save less as saving becomes less attractive compared to consumption. An alternative view is that they might save more in order to obtain a target level of income earned in interest. The relative importance of these reactions varies between individuals. In practice, the effect of an interest rate change is *lagged*.

A 1 per cent increase in deposit interest rates raises savings by 0.6 per cent after a one-quarter lag.

(c) *Inflation*: This affects the *real* value of interest rates. If consumers behave rationally then a rise in inflation and unchanged interest rates make savings less attractive from an income-generating point of view. This situation might also make consumption more attractive and so reduce the amount saved. However, the higher inflation has eroded the real value of already accumulated savings and if people have a target real value of savings they might save more rather than less at times of high inflation.

The savings of *firms* are effectively the profits retained in the business and not distributed to shareholders. They are likely to increase in economic boom times when company profits accrue more quickly.

It is not really appropriate to refer to government savings because the state is a net borrower. Each year since 1969 it has run a budget deficit. A budget surplus occurs when central government annual income exceeds annual expenditure, as in 1987–8.

This illustrates the precautionary effect. In 1973–5 savings increased at a time of rising inflation. A monetarist explanation of this phenomenon might be that people suffered the money illusion, being attracted by the high nominal interest rates (and not allowing for inflation).

See Chapter 6 Essential knowledge.

7.4.3 Investment

Investment is expenditure on *capital goods* of various sorts – fixed capital (e.g. machinery, houses), stocks of raw materials, work-in-progress and unsold but finished goods. Generally, the greater the capital stock of an economy, the more is the potential for growth. Three-quarters of all investment is undertaken by private sector and one-quarter by public sector.

In the simple Keynesian model, investment is assumed unrealistically to be constant. As such, it is unrelated to national income and equal to savings at the equilibrium level of national income.

A distinction is sometimes made between social and private investment. The former covers things such as roads and hospitals built for the benefit of the community as a whole, whereas private investment is undertaken to facilitate business and individual gain.

Planned and realized investment are only equal at the equilibrium level of national income.

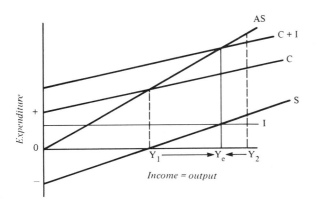

Figure 7.2 *Equilibrium national income*

Between Y_1 and Y_e investment exceeds savings and so *planned injections* exceed *planned leakages*. This causes national income to increase. The reverse happens at the disequilibrium position Y_2. There is unintended stock accumulation which leads to lower production and subsequently smaller national income, until equilibrium is restored.

The amount of investment undertaken by firms is determined by:

This is the opportunity cost of the investment.

(a)   Expectations about *future profit* flows. This means consideration of the likely revenue generated by the output (resulting from the investment) in comparison with the anticipated costs of the investment.

(b)   The *current valuation* which firms place on the likely future profits.

These factors form the basis of two investment theories – the marginal efficiency of capital theory and the discounted cash flow theory.

The marginal efficiency of capital was proposed by Keynes. The m.e.c. is the rate of interest necessary to make the present value of the income stream from the investment equal to the supply price of the investment. If the m.e.c. exceeds the current rate of interest then the investment is worth undertaking.

The m.e.c. is like a *demand* curve for investment. At a high current rate of interest the amount of investment is lower than at a low rate of interest. Keynesians see the rate of interest as a relatively unimportant determinant of investment, hence their m.e.c. is *interest inelastic*. The expected *yield* carries more weight than the rate of interest. It is determined by the state of business confidence, the substitutability of other factors and government policy.

An optimistic business, higher costs of possible substitute factors and encouraging government taxation policies all tend to push m.e.c. to the right. This makes investment more likely at existing current interest rates.

Q1 . . . Q4 are the anticipated yearly returns. r is rate of interest. N is number of years over which the returns are expected.

The *discounted cash flow* theory incorporated a formula to calculate the present value of the income stream from an investment.

$$PV = \frac{Q1}{(1+r)^1} + \frac{Q2}{(1+r)^2} + \frac{Q3}{(1+r)^3} \cdots \frac{Qn}{(1+r)^4}$$

The higher the rate of interest, the lower the PV and the less likely that the investment will take place. If the PV exceeds the supply price of the investment then the project should go ahead, other things being equal.

However, some of these *other things* may inhibit investment although they do not affect the yield and cost of an investment. For instance, if *credit* is not readily available then investment will not ensue. Alternatively, *new technical advances*, an *expanding market*, and a high level of *national income* will tend to create optimism in businesses which will stimulate investment.

In the early 1980s, public sector investment was curtailed in order to keep down public spending in line with monetarist economic policy. Britain now has the lowest investment in construction in Europe.

Public sector investment is less governed by yield and cost considerations and more concerned with social need and political desirability. However, nationalized industries abide by commercial principles, even though government departments are not subject to market influences.

7.4.4   *The accelerator and the multiplier*

These two ideas attempt to explain different relationships between investment and national income (and output).

The accelerator

The accelerator describes the effect of a *change in income* on investment spending. Assuming firms maintain a constant capital-output ratio, changes in final demand for goods will influence the amount of investment. Thus higher national income leads to higher demand which leads to new investment. However, if the *percentage increase* in income is not maintained there will be an absolute fall in investment, unless some existing machines need replacement. The production of investment goods is therefore even more cyclical than the production of consumer goods. For instance, a single change in demand can produce an echo effect on investment at regular intervals.

The accelerator has been criticized as oversimplified. In practice firms keep *stocks* to meet demand upsurges and retain *excess capacity* which can be utilized to raise output. In addition, obsolescence is usually well planned. In the British economy, a 1 per cent increase in manufacturing output results in a 2 per cent increase in investment after a fifteen-month time lag.

The multiplier

The multiplier describes the effect of an *injection*, such as investment, on *national income*. The initial increase in aggregate monetary demand is multiplied through the economy and the effect can be quantified, at least in theory. There are various multipliers but the usual complex model of the economy identifies three significant *leakages* – savings, taxation and imports – which gives a formula for the multiplier (k):

$$K = \frac{1}{MP_s + MP_t + MP_m}$$

Whatever the model:

$$K = \frac{1}{\text{marginal rate of leakage} - \text{the marginal rate of injection}}$$

Generally, the lower the size of the multiplier, the less scope there is for government intervention to influence national income.

Even a *balanced budget* can have a multiplier effect. This happens because a tax increase eventually reduces national income by less than the corresponding spending increase. The multiplier impact of budget changes varies between measures. For instance, higher state benefits have a greater income-generating effect than top rate income tax reductions because the recipients of the former have higher MPCs than the latter and so likely leakages are lower.

Keynesians support public works schemes particularly because they can be directly targeted and largely avoid import leakages. However, monetarists dislike budget deficits because they pre-empt private sector resources and (they argue that) they raise prices rather than output, through money supply effects.

7.4.5 *Quantity theory of money*

This theory underpins monetarism. It is based on the equation of exchange:

$$MV = PT$$

For a more detailed explanation, combined with calculated example, refer to Chapter 19 of Economics for Accountants.

The echo occurs at the end of the life span of the original investment when replacements are required.

In the non-manufacturing private sector (e.g. hotels) the increase in investment has been greater. This has been particularly true since 1982 when manufacturing investment started only a slow recovery (because of business pessimism, high nominal and real interest rates, falling net rates of return and excess capacity caused by 1979–81 recession).

The higher the marginal propensities, the lower the multiplier e.g. $MPS = 0.1$, $MPT = 0.3$, $MP_m = 0.2$, $K = \frac{1}{0.6} = 1.66$.
So an initial injection of £100 million increases national income by £166 million.

The reason being that savings are lowered by a tax increase and consumption decisions are made out of post-tax income.

M = money supply, v = velocity of circulation, p = average price, t = total number of transactions. T is equivalent to total output. In a more modern version of the equation Y (real national income) replaces T.

Monetarists assume that *v* and *t* are *constant* in the short run and so a change in money supply determines the price level. Keynesians dispute the assumptions and suggest a different sequence of causation. They argue that the money supply adapts to changes in demand at current prices.

The monetarist argument is that the *demand for money* is *stable*, being mainly for transactions purposes, and is raised by an increase in the supply of money. The excess demand is spent but this raises prices rather than output. Prices rise because there is an increase in demand for all goods and services, including financial assets. Furthermore, some monetarists argue that price cannot change independently of the money supply.

Some Keynesians would even argue that a change in the velocity of circulation can change prices, irrespective of changes in the money supply.

Keynesians argue that *v* may not be constant, as people may spend their money more quickly if money supply does not change. More significantly, they perceive a different transmission mechanism. Although they accept that an increase in money supply might lead to inflation, they claim that there is a different sequence of causation. The money supply adapts to *changes in the demand for money*. In addition Keynesians believe that demand is *elastic*, as money could be held for speculative motives so that an interest rate change could be seized upon. They make a further criticism of the quantity theory in that they argue that an expansion of the money supply could increase output, rather than prices.

In the twentieth century the velocity of circulation has varied between 1.5 and 3.2, ranging between 2.5–3.1 in 1970s and 1980s.

Evidence from research helps neither school of thought. The identification of short-run fluctuations in the velocity of circulation undermines the monetarist assumptions, and the difficulties of measuring and controlling the money supply have cast doubt on their description of the transmission mechanism. Empirical evidence also suggests that the demand for money is fairly interest inelastic, thereby querying Keynesian assumptions. However, the demand for money does appear to be exogenously determined, as Keynesians claim.

See Chapter 5.

Bank of England 1965–80 data gave demand for money – 0.29.

7.4.6   *Policy instruments*

Various methods are used by governments to reach targets in the pursuit of broader objectives. Monetarists have little faith though in discretionary economic management by governments. They advocate *fixed policy rules* and *target setting* e.g. money supply growth target ranges but trust to market solutions. Once the targets have been set then the government should not tinker, as this will distort market behaviour which has been formulated in the light of the government's policy pronouncements.

The acceptable government intervention to monetarists is in making *markets more competitive*. This means removing restrictive practices and other *supply side* deficiencies so that rigidities are reduced and efficiency is stimulated. For instance, the 1980s trade union laws limiting their bargaining strength. This philosophy has made monetarists oppose *incomes policy* which some Keynesians advocate. Monetarists are also sceptical of the value of fiscal policy, which Keynesians prefer, and use it in conjunction with *monetary policy* which they deem to be more important.

Keynesians ascribe to the government an important role in macro-economics, using different policy instruments to achieve the main economic objectives. They favour the discretionary use of *fiscal policy* to correct market instability. For instance, if unemployment was high then Keynesians would loosen the fiscal stance in order to raise aggregate monetary demand. This policy has been attacked by monetarists for producing high inflation. It has also been criticized for incurring balance of payments problems which then lead to the policy reversal of a tighter fiscal stance and subsequent deflation.

Balance of payments difficulties resulted from increased spending on imports when AMD expanded.

However, Keynesians would supplement fiscal policy with a monetary policy. In seeking to raise AMD, the monetary weapons of lower interest rates and more freely available credit could be used. The primary purpose of monetary policy though was to manage the *national debt*, varying interest rates to suit *funding* requirements. Monetarists abhor such a discretionary approach.

Keynesians would use fiscal policy to attain employment and growth objectives but recognized its limitations regarding inflation and the balance of payments. *Incomes policy* was utilized in the late 1960s and 1970s to curb inflation, but it has lost credence since. However, it is generally agreed that wage and price controls can work for a period of time if the policy is firmly applied. After a while though criticisms intensify and government resolve weakens so that in subsequent non-incomes policy periods wages accelerate and inflation reappears.

Some groups may be given 'special awards' because either they have a just case or they have industrial muscle, and these deals undermine the comprehensive coverage and equal ethos which is the strength of incomes policy.

The balance of payments objective has been more elusive than most. In the 1960s *devaluation* was proposed as a means of restoring a payments equilibrium. It did not have the undesirable impact on unemployment which deflation had. This policy option disappeared with the regime of *floating exchange rates* from 1971. Subsequently, some Keynesians have advocated import controls, behind which British industry could be regenerated. However, because of the EEC and GATT implications of such a policy, generally less direct methods of intervention have been used. An *exchange rate policy* is acceptable to Keynesians because they believe in the value of government manipulation. They would have an exchange rate *target* for the Bank of England to attain. This would require *dirty floating*. In theory, monetarists should oppose such action as it distorts the market. However, the desire to curb inflation has meant that some monetarists have accepted the need to push the pound down and thereby restrain import prices. Similarly a floating exchange rate may make governments *less disciplined* in their monetary policy and lead to reckless reflation, when they rely on the exchange rate to maintain equilibrium on the balance of payments.

The 'siege economy' package also included withdrawal from the EEC but this option is less credible nowadays.

Dirty floating occurs when the Bank of England buys (or sells) pounds in order to raise (or decrease) the exchange rate towards the desired target figure. Generally, a lower exchange rate makes exports relatively cheaper and imports more expensive.

Chancellor Lawson since 1986 has supported such thinking.

7.4.7 *Keynesian demand management*

Keynesians give governments a positive role to play in an economy, believing that markets do not naturally reach equilibrium and so involuntary unemployment may arise. Their approach is to influence the major components of aggregate monetary demand in order to achieve the prevailing major economic objective.

This presents the effective use of resources in the economy as some labour is not utilized productively.

$AMD = C + I + G.$

If other things such as taxation were unchanged then higher government spending would mean a laxer fiscal stance.

Demand pull inflation.

In Figure 7.3 at AMD and Y_1 there is equilibrium. However, this equilibrium is not necessarily compatible with full employment and price stability. If Y_2 is a level of output securing *full employment* then Keynesians would raise the G component and thus AMD. However, if the fiscal boost increased spending to AMD_3 then the excess demand would create an inflationary gap. This *inflation* could be removed by lowering spending, through higher taxes to reduce consumption or curtail government spending, to AMD_2. Such a deflationary policy gave rise to the 'stop-go' economic management which was criticized as a cause of Britain's poor rate of economic growth in the post-war period. Only at AMD_2 and Y_2 is there an equilibrium with both inflation and employment objectives fulfilled. Such achievement requires excellent timing in using policy instruments, up-to-date knowledge of the economy, accurate understanding of the interrelationships between the main economic variables and no extraneous trade shocks.

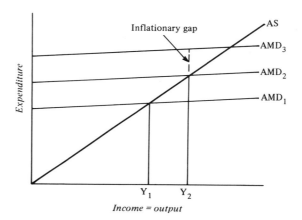

Figure 7.3   *Inflation in a Keynesian model*

National income is plotted against prices, rather than expenditure.

However, the conjunction of inflation and rising unemployment has led to a modified model. In this model AMD is downward sloping and aggregate supply becomes more inelastic as the full employment level of national income is approached.

In Figure 7.4, the expansion in the economy Y_1–Y_2 can be achieved with little inflation P_1–P_2, as unemployed resources are utilized. However,

This cost increase has been caused by excess demand and so is determined endogenously.

Y_3–Y_f progress results in high inflation P_s–P_4, both proportionately and relatively. The higher costs of production which cause the inflation could result from either the price of these scarce resources being bid upon from their relative inefficiency (as more efficient resources are purchased first). Thus between Y_f–Y_y there is rising inflation and significant unemployment.

This model also provides for a shift in the aggregate supply curve, which can occur when *cost push* inflation occurs. If aggregate demand remains unchanged, a new equilibrium will be achieved at a lower output and a higher rate of inflation. In Figure 7.4 AS_c shows the supply after cost push

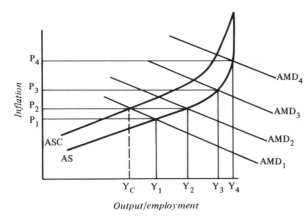

Figure 7.4 *A modified Keynesian model*

inflation with the resultant fall in output/employment to Y_c and the increase in inflation to P_2.

7.4.8 *Phillips curves*

The monetarist analysis of the interrelationship between inflation and unemployment involves a resuscitated Phillips curve. The original Phillips curve correlated changes in UK *money wages* and *unemployment* between 1861 and 1957. As shown in Figure 7.5, if unemployment was 5½ per cent then money wages would not change; while at 2½ per cent money wages would increase in line with productivity and so be non-inflationary. An explanation for the correlation was that workers obtained higher wages when employers were short-staffed and markets were borrowing and that these conditions only occurred at times of low unemployment. The Phillips curve showed a *trade-off* between inflation, through the proxy of money wages, and unemployment.

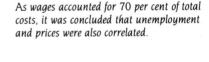

As wages accounted for 70 per cent of total costs, it was concluded that unemployment and prices were also correlated.

This tradeoff meant that the full employment objective and the price stability objective were mutually exclusive.

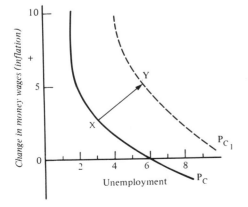

Figure 7.5 *Phillips curve*

However, in the late 1960s the rates of inflation and unemployment began to move in the same direction and the original *Phillips curve was discredited.* It was argued that the level of unemployment was no longer a good indicator of excess demand because of the increase in female activity rates, higher unemployment benefits and the black economy. Also, trade unions' increased power resulted in higher wage inflation at each level of unemployment. Defenders of the Phillips curve philosophy accepted the impact of these social and structural changes but simply argued that the *curve* had *shifted* to the right. In Figure 7.5, PC_1 shows the relationship at higher rates. Thus a movement from X to Y illustrates both higher inflation and higher unemployment.

A more recent *modification* distinguished between short-run and long-run Phillips curves. The existence of several potential Phillips curves meant that the negative interrelationship between inflation and unemployment was not permanent. In the short run it was possible but the *long-run Phillips curve was vertical,* passing through the *natural rate of unemployment* (U_1 in Figure 7.6). This occurred when the labour market was in equilibrium and price rises, both actual and expected, were zero. The natural rate of unemployment therefore included frictional and structural but not demand-deficient unemployment.

The most common theory incorporating the natural rate of unemployment and price expectations is the *expectations-augmented Phillips curve.* Friedman shows that if governments intervene to keep unemployment artificially low, by Keynesian demand management policies, then a period of severe unemployment will be necessary to shake inflationary expectations out of the system.

In Figure 7.6 if a government reduces unemployment to U when there is no inflation (P_{e_0}) the excess demand results in 5 per cent inflation. This raises price expectations and shifts the short-run Phillips curve to P_{e_s}. Unemployment will increase from U to U_1 because some employed will quit

These factors all suggested that unemployment would be higher than before at each level of inflation.

This also ties in with cost push theory. It argues that strong trade unions, even at times of rising unemployment, can obtain high wage increases which are passed on through administered prices in uncompetitive markets. Unfortunately, there is little empirical evidence that trade union pushfulness is an exogenously determined cause of inflation. However, world commodity prices are such a cause and Beckerman's research plausibly supports their significance.

Monetarists do not recognize demand deficient unemployment and regard unemployment at the natural rate as involuntary.

This assumes excess demand leading to higher wages leading to increased inflation; and that there are no productivity improvements.

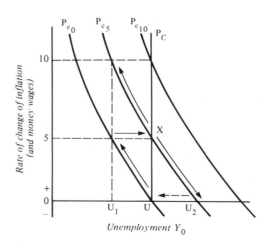

Figure 7.6   *The expectations-augmented Phillips curve*

their jobs realizing that real wages have not risen while there will be a fall in employers' demand for labour.

However, if a government persists in keeping relatively *low* unemployment (i.e. U_1f inflationary expectations will accelerate along the P_{e_s} curve to 10 per cent. This occurs because wage bargainers, after suffering the *money illusion*, realize that higher wages are needed to obtain real wage increases.

The government can *stabilize inflation* by accepting the prevailing rate of unemployment and maintaining the growth of demand in line with the current rate of inflation. This makes actual and expected rates of inflation the same at a level acceptable to the government. In the long run, this gives a vertical long-run Phillips curve.

The money illusion arises when people do not allow for the effects of inflation when making economic decisions. For instance, a 5 per cent increase in money wages is a fall in real wages if inflation exceeds 5 per cent.

If the government decides to *lower inflation* it needs to reduce inflationary expectations. At X with 5 per cent inflation a reduction in money supply of 5 per cent causes excess supply in the economy and makes expected inflation above actual inflation. These combine to raise unemployment to U_2. Eventually, expectations of inflation are lowered to zero, wage settlements fall and there is increased demand for labour which reduces unemployment to the natural rate (U).

Employers faced with falling prices and lower demand lay off workers.

Expectations hold a central place in this economic model being derived from past experience. The *rational-expectations* hypothesis has a different emphasis. It assumes rational behaviour by economic agents. The government, by its behaviour, can set examples and thereby influence expectations in the economy. This could produce lower inflation without higher unemployment i.e. a movement down the long-run Phillips curve. In practice, some economic behaviour and much expectation is not that rational. This tends to undermine the validity of the long-run Phillips curve.

The money supply targets in the medium term financial strategy were such examples. The hope was that workers might settle for smaller wage rises, safe in the knowledge that inflation would fall because of money supply controls, and thereby actually produce the lower inflation.

The natural rate of unemployment is *not fixed*. Although government macroeconomic policy cannot permanently alter it, according to the monetarists, labour market changes can affect the natural rate. A government through microeconomic policies can influence market conditions e.g. removing trade union restrictive practices.

Other measures such as lower unemployment benefits and better job opportunity information tend to make the supply of labour more elastic.

The non-accelerating inflation rate of unemployment (NAIRU) has evolved from the expectations-augmented Phillips curve. NAIRU is reached when inflation stabilizes, and extra unemployment has no impact on prices. The idea is more acceptable to Keynesians as it includes *involuntary* as well as *voluntary* unemployment.

Estimates of NAIRU for Britain have been revised upward from 4.0 per cent (1971–5) to 9.2 per cent (1981–3). This happened because the *demand* for labour *fell* and *supply* remained fairly *inelastic*. Labour's poor productivity and rising real wages made them less attractive, while squeezed profit margins deterred employers from recruitment. Trade union power, narrow wage differentials, labour immobility and unemployment benefits steady in real terms all contributed towards the supply of labour's failure to become more elastic. Even in the 1980s as inflation has been significantly reduced *real wages have increased*, despite high unemployment. It could be argued that even higher unemployment,

9.2 per cent was below the actual unemployment in that period of 10.8 per cent suggesting that unemployment could be lowered without causing inflation. This suggests unemployment could move from U2 to U in Figure 7.6.

In 1986–7 average wage increases at 7.7 per cent outpaced inflation at 3.7 per cent.

above NAIRU, might be needed in future if inflation starts to increase again. Some economists, particularly Keynesians, argue that deflationary policies and even higher unemployment will have little effect on wages partly because the long-term unemployed do not act as a constraint on trade union bargainers.

The recent scepticism over the Phillips curve relationship and the increase in real wages for 87 per cent of the workforce have provoked criticisms of the natural rate and NAIRU. Layard and Nickel have proposed that it is the *rate of change of unemployment* rather than the absolute level which influences wage bargainers. Thus, once unemployment levels off, trade unions no longer moderate wage claims and this might stimulate inflation again. A corollary of this is that general reflation combined with industry's lack of capacity will have the same upward effect on wages and prices. Ironically, although a lack of demand in the economy precipitated a lot of the unemployment, a reflation would probably have little impact on unemployment because of increased productivity and growing real wages.

It has been suggested, particularly by Conservative governments, that American unemployment since 1980 has fallen because *real wages* did not increase. However, critics of this view point to Reagan's *relaxed fiscal stance* (combined with a strict monetary policy) which contributed to output growth.

The long-term unemployed are becoming a larger proportion of the total. This has prompted government initiatives, such as the Restart and Community Project schemes, aimed specifically at reducing the numbers of long-term unemployed. This might indirectly make trade unions less pushful and supply more elastic.

This theory fits the recent real wage changes which were relatively low in 1980–2, but higher since 1983.

The workfare scheme and lower unemployment benefits have made labour supply more elastic and thereby held down labour costs. Hence microeconomic policies in Britain to reduce trade union influence and reduce state benefits in real terms have been tried.

Revision questions

1 What are the functions of the Bank of England?   (CIMA May 1987)

2 'A commercial banker's role is to convert illiquid assets into usable credit.'
   (a) Explain this statement and state why this role is important.
   (b) What limits a banker's ability to create credit?

(CIMA May 1986)

8
International trade

8.1 Topic relationship

The ideas, issues and information in this chapter are closely related to those of the two preceding chapters. This chapter considers the relationships between *external trade* and the *domestic economy*. For instance, a world economic depression, as occurred 1980–1, has internal repercussions. It can affect governmental objectives regarding employment and growth. Similarly, a massive increase in imports can weaken the balance of payments account and indirectly lower the value of the exchange rate.

The 1980–1 world depression contributed significantly to the rapid increase in unemployment at that time and the negative growth rate.

The development of *international institutions* and *trading organizations* has affected macroeconomic aggregates and government decision making. Individual governments are less sovereign now than in the past. They heed international pressure and sometimes acknowledge the needs of others.

Membership of the IMF has influenced British government behaviour, notably in 1976–7 when the Labour government applied some of the IMF's recommended economic ideas as a condition of securing a loan to support the exchange rate. On a more permanent basis Britain's membership of the EEC has caused a *redistribution of income* from taxpayers and consumers to farmers.

This redistribution has occurred because farmers have received higher prices, helped by subsidies derived from government policies.

The underlying basis for international trade is similar to that of domestic trade. The participants seek a mutual increase in *welfare*. The exchange which occurs requires a *medium of exchange*. However, payment difficulties are more likely to arise at an international level because of the vicissitudes in world currency market. Similarly, deliberately imposed restrictions such as *tariff barriers* may curtail trading activity.

World trade is dominated by the advanced industrial nations, led by USA, Japan and West Germany. However, the *world economy* is fraught with major *problems*. There is no one currency which can act as an anchor and there is no method for agreeing appropriate policies for promoting the growth of world living standards. Also, a *North–South divide* has evolved. The 'North' refers to the industrialized nations, which are mainly North European and American, and the 'South' refers to the less developed nations which congregate south of the equator in Africa, Asia and South America.

This contrasts with an individual nation's economy where the currency is settled and a government decides on the appropriate policies.

8.2   Underlying concepts

Economies *specialize* in the same way as companies do. This specialization benefits the world economy, because it enables the differing resources and skills of nations to gain the advantages of the *division of labour*. Economies of scale can be obtained and lower prices created.

Britain leads the world in provision of financial services.

If world trade is free, without restrictions, then there will be *competition* which should ultimately benefit consumers through greater choice and lower prices. However, because some nations, or certain industries, lose in competitive markets *trade barriers* have been developed for protection.

The theory of *comparative* advantage demonstrates the gains from specialization and free trade. Even where one nation has an absolute advantage in producing the same two goods as another country, it pays to specialize.

It has simplifying assumptions that two economies each produce the same two goods and that the factors of production are perfectly mobile. Furthermore there are no trade barriers, no transport costs and no changes in technology.

If opportunity cost ratios are the same, there is no benefit from specialization and trade. In Table 8.1 the ratios are 5 ÷ 4 in A and 9 ÷ 1 in B.

Table 8.1   Comparative advantage

Country	Initial production		After specialization		With partial specialization		After trade	
	X	Y	X	Y	X	Y	X	Y
A	100	80	–	160	40	128	130	98
B	90	10	180	–	180	–	90	30
World total	190	90	180	160	220	128	220	128

In Table 8.1 if A devotes all its resources to the manufacture of Y where it is relatively more efficient and B solely produces X then the total world output increases to 340 from 280. But, this gives fewer world Xs and more Ys. However, if A devotes some of its resources to making X and the rest to producing Y, then more of both X and Y globally can be manufactured. In Table 8.1 the partial specialization illustrates this position.

In addition to transport and peace, international trade requires *exchange rates*. An exchange rate is the *external price* of a currency. In theory, these reflect the cost of resources used and are limited by the *opportunity cost* ratios of production. In Table 8.1 country A would value Y = 5/4X while B would value Y = 9X and so an exchange value between these two extremes would be expected so that both A and B could benefit. If the exchange rate were 3X = Y, A could sell 30Y to B and receive 90X in return. The 'after trade' column of Table 8.1 shows the final post-trade position which reveals mutual gains compared with the first column. From trade, A has gained 30X and 18Y while B has benefited with 20 more Y.

The opportunity cost ratios which indicate relative prices are the basis of the *terms of trade*.

The ratio has 100 in its base year. It is an increasingly less useful statistic as it only refers to trade in goods, and factors other than the price affect international demand too.

This concept no longer just refers to the ratio of one good to another. In the real world the terms of trade are based on *weighted indices* showing average price changes when all traded goods are considered. The index of export prices divided by the index of import prices × 100 per cent gives terms of trade index number. A rise indicates an improvement and means that export prices are rising faster than import prices.

Changes in the terms of trade and exchange rates affect the *balance of payments*. This account shows the financial transactions of one nation with the rest of the world over a period of time. Since Spring 1987 it has been presented as follows:

Current account	
Visibles	
Invisibles	‾
Current balance	A
UK external assets and liabilities	‾
Transactions in assets	‾
Transactions in liabilities	+
Net transactions	B
Balancing item	C

Visibles equal trade in goods. Frequently in deficit, except for oil and gas earnings 1979–83. Invisibles equal trade in services. Usually in surplus as a result of interest, profits and dividends earned abroad; and the financial services offered by the City of London. The main deficits items in this section of the accounts are the transfers by governments and private individuals.

The new format emphasizes the current balance, which is the main statistic in the accounts and removes the distinction between the capital account and official financing. The *balancing item* ensures that the balance of payments always balances because $A+B+C$ sums to zero. A positive balancing item indicates unrecorded exports and occurs most commonly in Britain's case. Frequent, large balancing items show the problems of *information gathering* and the reliance on *estimates*, particularly for invisibles. *Revisions* to previously published figures are not uncommon. The *reserves* are included under transactions in assets.

The transactions section of the accounts comprises all public and private capital movements. The assets and liabilities include both real and paper investments.

A persistent imbalance, particularly in the current balance, indicates a *fundamental disequilibrium*. Usually, a continuing deficit is of more concern to a government than a regular surplus. Such a deficit demonstrates an *uncompetitiveness* in trade. In Britain's case, *import penetration*, particularly in manufactured goods in the early 1980s, has been the main cause of such disequilibrium. The proportion of UK market taken by manufactured imports increased from one-quarter to one-third between 1980–5. In contrast the *export sales ratio* in manufacturing only marginally increased (27 per cent to 30 per cent).

For example in March 1986, the 1984 invisible surplus was raised from £4.3 billion to £5.3 billion.

The visible trade deficits indicated Britain's comparative disadvantage in goods but the invisibles surplus showed the comparative advantage in the provision of services.

This is illustrated vividly by motor vehicles. In 1970 7 per cent of British new cars came from Japan and Europe, while in 1986 57 per cent were imported.

8.3   Points of perspective

International trade is more vital to Britain than most other economies because of its trading heritage. The economy is heavily *dependent* on imports of food and fuels which are not indigenous. In addition, Britain's economy is also very *open* and this relative lack of tariffs makes it susceptible to changes in the world economy. Although EEC membership gives Britain more *protection* from non-EEC goods, it opens up British markets to European competitors. As a result, Britain's main trading partner is now *West Germany*, rather than USA.

Britain has been a leading member of many international bodies and thus at the forefront of developments in world co-operation. Recent developments have been less formalized, though, as in the agreements

For example GATT and its attempts since 1947 to reduce tariffs and eliminate quotas. These have also been objectives of the IMF but it has pursued exchange rate stability, the ending of exchange controls and the lending of reserves as indirectly instrumental policies.

made by the group of seven finance ministers in 1987, the Louvre Accord tried to establish *greater stability* amongst the major currencies. Although the agreement was secret, it appeared that there was to be co-operation in dirty floating. This involved central banks in buying/selling a currency in order to raise/depress its exchange rate.

Exchange rate stability was necessary so that governments could exert greater influence over their own inflation and nominal interest rates. *Floating* exchange rates since 1971 had rendered such influence illusory. Furthermore, the increased flow of *hot money* had proved beyond the control of central banks when they intervened to manipulate exchange rates. The fact that *capital flows* account for 90 per cent of foreign exchange market dealings means that much of the traditional thinking regarding exchange rates has become invalid.

This is the familiar dilemma facing governments. The conflict between policy objectives and instruments is discussed in Chapter 7.

The purchase of currency for trade now has little effect on the exchange rate. This has weakened the link between the *exchange rate and the balance of payments*. In the past, a payments deficit tended to depress the exchange rate but now other factors have greater significance i.e. *interest rate differentials*, the faith of speculators in a government's anti-inflation policies and an economy's dependence on oil.

A rise in nominal interest rates could cause an exchange rate to appreciate despite a payments deficit.

North Sea Oil has made a significant impact on the British economy in the last decade, although only accounting for 5 per cent of GDP. In a direct way, the oil receipts have boosted the balance of payments earnings. Indirectly they have raised the status of *sterling* and perhaps made it artificially more desirable. Interestingly, between mid-1982 and early 1987 the pound–deutschemark exchange rate followed a very similar pattern to the spot oil price pinpointing sterling as a petro-currency.

However, the indirect effect in the short term has been an accentuated deindustrialization. In the long run though, if the oil surpluses have been effectively used then investment abroad will boost invisible earnings while investment at home will generate greater economic growth.

8.4   Essential knowledge

8.4.1   *Free trade and protection*

Free trade which encourages specialization enables the world economy to increase its total production. The benefits of *competition*, the *division of labour*, *economies of scale* and increased *choice* can accrue.

However, free trade theory and practice diverge. There are some practical *constraints* on *international trade*:

In the long run factors, particularly labour, through retraining, can become more mobile.

(a)   *Factors are not perfectly mobile*: This may prevent extensive specialization, particularly in the short run.

(b)   *Markets may be inaccessible*: Some markets may be naturally remote while others may be artificially protected. In these circumstances full specialization cannot be achieved and so would be potentially wasteful as production would not be sold.

Generally transport costs are falling thereby opening up more markets e.g. British imports of coal are increasing.

(c)   *The costs of transport*: The simplifying assumption of no transport costs is unrealistic, and transport does limit market size.

(d)   *Trade restrictions*: These may be imposed for economic, social and political reasons.

For example US limitations on trade in technology with communist countries.

The welfare of each nation in the world economy depends upon how the benefits of world trade are distributed. One nation may feel that it is in its self interest to restrict the freedom of trade. *Protection* occurs for various reasons:

(a) *To prevent 'unfair' competition*: Fake goods and dumping are two practices which could be deemed as unfair. Also, subsidies to exporters may give their goods an unfair advantage.

(b) *To help an infant industry*: Sunrise industries have been protected until they are strong enough to compete with established international rivals.

(c) *To protect domestic employment*: Localized unemployment may result from successive foreign competition (e.g. textiles) when a comparative advantage is lost and factors are immobile.

(d) *To protect the balance of payments*: Import penetration weakens balance of payments current account and so trade restrictions would strengthen balance of payments by lowering imports and persuading consumers to buy the more available British goods.

(e) *To maintain security*: Essential military goods may be produced at home even when foreign goods are more efficient so that the government maintains political control.

The main *arguments against protection* are that:

(a) *Inefficiency is encouraged*: Because the protected British firms may settle for an easy life and not fully utilize their factors of production.

(b) *Resources are misallocated*: Because they remain in their existing use, even as its profitability declines.

(c) *The cost of living increases*: Because tariffs raise import prices while quotas push consumers into buying the probably more expensive British goods.

(d) *Welfare gains will be lost*: Because the benefits of specialization – trade – exchange do not arise.

(e) *Retaliation may occur*: Because other nations may introduce protection thereby lowering the volume of world trade.

The main trade barriers used are *tariffs* which act on the *price* of goods and services and *quotas* which restrict the *quantity* of imports. A more acceptable (to GATT) and modern form of protection is the *voluntary export restraint agreement* (VERA). This limits the amount of a specific good after negotiation with the exporting nation e.g Japanese cars in Britain limited to 12 per cent market share.

There are also *administrative controls* used by some countries subtly to undermine foreign competition e.g. complex procedures, complicated forms, unusual product specifications. All of which favour domestic suppliers and work against imports. Home producers are also helped by *public procurement* in some strategic industries, *export subsidies* and *cheap export credits*.

It has been suggested that a new era of protectionism began in 1973. The *new protectionism* was characterized by these modern trade barriers, agricultural subsidies and the increased use of *bi-lateral trade agreements*.

Fake imitations may break patent laws and be potentially harmful e.g. hairspray.

Dumping refers to the selling of exports at very low prices often to get a toehold in a market e.g. Japanese excavators.

The 'temporary' multifibre agreement of 1975 to restrict cheap imported textiles into Europe is still operational.

In Britain's case they are unlikely to be introduced because of the Conservative government's faith in the market and our international treaty obligations.

In 1987 the government controversially bought the American AWACS rather than the British NIMROD. However, this was probably the exception which proves the rule!

From a world perspective, such protection means the principle of comparative advantage in the production of low-quality manufactured goods because of their cheap labour.

Higher prices lower the consumer surplus.

Such declines tend to provoke depressions and growing unemployment in most advanced nations.

These subsidies make exports either cheaper or more desirable and so constitute an unfair advantage. The USA vehemently criticizes the EEC's subsidy to its steel.

Britain and Turkey have an agreement over T-shirt imports.

These developments have caused friction between governments and friction between governments and trading blocs. They have also undermined GATT and intensified the North–South divide by discriminating against low-cost suppliers.

The growth of trading blocs, such as the *EEC*, has ironically increased free trade *and* protection. The member states enjoy *free trade* but a *common external tariff* is levied on imports to the customs union. In addition, the EEC's *common agricultural policy* which is organized to eliminate large fluctuations in farm prices protects its farmers from outside competition.

Another major influential organization on world trade has been *OPEC*. This cartel of oil suppliers has exerted control over oil prices, notably in 1973 and 1979, and thereby precipitated worldwide economic depressions because of the dependence of most advanced economies on imported oil.

8.4.2 British trade

Most of Britain's trade is in semi-manufactured and engineering goods with the *EEC*. Britain's main individual trading partner is now West Germany, rather than the USA. However, the trade in services is growing significantly, although this again is concentrated in Europe and North America.

In Figure 8.1 the trade in goods is shown by value. It confirms the *import penetration* in manufactured goods and the relative importance of *fuel exports*. The historical picture of Britain mainly importing food, fuel and raw materials and exporting predominantly manufactured goods is no longer very accurate. The low income elasticity of demand for food and Britain's stable population explain the relative decline of food imports. Although Figure 8.1 shows the relative importance of each sector it must not be forgotten that export *values*, allowing for inflation, increase yearly.

The developing nations often have a comparative advantage in the production of low-quality manufactured goods because of their cheap labour.

Resources are wasted because surplus crops are stored e.g. in 1985 half of Britain's grain harvest went into store. The British cost of such intervention exceeds £1.3 billion annually.

Since 1979 OPEC's unity has been fragmented by Britain's unilateral behaviour, the Iran–Iraq war and international squabbles over supply quotas. In 1986 oil prices fell from $30 to $10 per barrel.

Oil and gas from the North Sea.

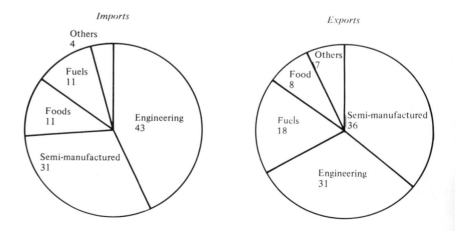

Figure 8.1 *British trade 1985 by commodity*

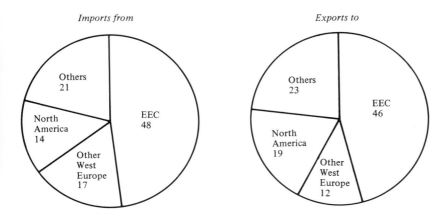

Figure 8.2   *British trade 1985 by area*

Nevertheless, Britain has lost some key export markets by its concentration on *low-value goods*, poor quality and lack of price-competitiveness.

Geographically, Britain's trade is dominated by *Europe*, with EEC share increasing since Britain's 1973 entry. This move was probably beneficial though. Economic growth and export performance have both improved since entry, although inflation is slightly higher through CAP and there is a budget transfer to EEC funds. The emergence of *North Sea Oil* and the decline of the *Commonwealth* have altered Britain's trade patterns so that she has fewer OPEC and Commonwealth imports.

Britain's fastest-growing single trading partner is Japan, with whom there is a deficit on goods trade but a surplus on services. This partnership has extended to joint production e.g. BL Honda and Japanese plants in Britain e.g. Nissan on Tyneside, making Japan the second-largest investor behind America in Britain.

8.4.3   Balance of payments

When a *fundamental disequilibrium* arises, policy action is needed to restore equilibrium. However, remedial action may undermine attempts to achieve *other economic objectives*. For instance, deflation to cut consumption on imports will slow down economic growth and increase unemployment.

Britain's 1970s deficits on current account stemmed from *uncompetitiveness* which facilitated import penetration. The main causes of this have been *higher unit costs* and *non-price factors* such as poor design, unreliability and delayed delivery. These factors have also contributed to Britain's insufficient export performance. In addition, British *exports* are *price inelastic* in the short run and face much lower income elasticities abroad.

In the early 1980s North Sea Oil and Gas enabled Britain to obtain current account surpluses. However, these were only temporary and

Unlike the Japanese, British producers have not moved sufficiently up market to provide luxurious consumer durables as the standard of living continues to rise.

Australia and New Zealand dairy and meat exports to Britain suffered significantly with British EEC membership, whereas France and Netherlands gained.

The advantage of British plants to the Japanese is that the goods sell in Europe without bearing the EEC tariff.

On visibles, rather than invisibles.

Britain has a high income elasticity of demand for imports (=1.8) meaning that improvements in living standards cause imports to be sucked in.

It has been calculated that the short run price elasticity is greater than 0.5 but after two years probably increases to over 1.5.

The current account surpluses boosted the money supply and exchange rate, thereby decreasing competitiveness via (possibly) higher inflation and higher priced exports. However, many foreign assets were bought and the income generated by them could boost future invisible earnings, e.g. £4 billion per annum (LBS forecast).

underlying weaknesses, such as the reliance on *imported raw materials*, concentration on *down-market products* and the *openness* of the economy have led some economists to suggest that Britain has a *structural disequilibrium*.

Many different policy options have been advocated to help the balance of payments. Governments need quick results, for political reasons often, and so some of the measures are *short term. Keynesians* believe that government tinkering can have an impact whereas *monetarists* are sceptical. They prefer to set policy rules and trust the *market*; but Keynesians would argue, as we have seen in this chapter, that international trade has few of the characteristics of perfect competition.

The most commonly discussed policies have been:

(a) *Lowering domestic demand for imports*:   Deflation through either a tight fiscal policy or a restrictive monetary policy, or both, *lowers consumption* and cuts the demand for imports. Hopefully domestic firms faced with a stagnant home market will export. The side-effects of deflation make it undesirable. It causes higher unemployment and lower growth because the impact falls on output. Any balance of payments gain from deflation will be temporary and so it is unpopular.

Governments are reluctant to deflate and do not like to admit that their policies are deflationary, e.g. Conservative government 1980–2, cuts in public expenditure.

Before 1972 when exchange rates were fixed, this was called 'devaluation'.

(b) *Depreciating the exchange rate*:   A downward float of the exchange rate, induced by a central bank's *dirty floating*, will make exports cheaper and imports dearer. Thus British goods would become more competitive. The effectiveness of such an expenditure-switching policy depends on the *price elasticities of demand* for imports and exports. The Marshall-Lerner analysis requires the combined demand elasticities to exceed 1.0 for the balance of payments to gain. However, the elasticities approach ignores *non-price influences* on demand, *income effects* and the *supply side* of the equation. Even with favourable elasticities, depreciation may initially worsen the accounts – the '*J curve effect*'. This occurs because supply does not immediately respond to the increased demand and so the same quantity of goods is sold but at lower prices. If *supply* remains *inelastic* then a depreciation will have a negative effect. The central bank can also influence the exchange rate by its manipulation of *interest rates*. A fall in interest rates would depress demand for the currency and thus cause a depreciation. The admission in 1987 that the government had an exchange rate target, which it sought to maintain, means that flexible variations in the exchange rate are probably no longer a policy option for a Conservative government.

The elasticities are difficult to calculate. Generally Britain's export elasticity is low (0.5) but it does increase to over 1.0 after four years. Similarly the import elasticity is low (0.4).

An optimistic 'J' curve with more elastic supply gives B of P gains after nine months, lasting for at least one and a half years.

In the 1980s the main objective has been inflation control and so exchange rate appreciations have been desired to keep import prices lower.

For example £1 = $1.60.

See previous section – Arguments against protection.

(c) *Controlling imports*:   Tariffs and quotas cause *expenditure reduction* rather than switching but do not address the basic weakness of uncompetitiveness, except by temporary protection. *Selective controls* have been introduced e.g. textiles and *bi-lateral agreements* made but widespread action has economic disadvantages and political problems, given Britain's membership of EEC and GATT. Again the protectionist approach is essentially short term, although its proponents argue that British industry could be resurrected behind tariff walls so that it is much stronger in world markets when the tariffs are lifted. This resurrection would entail greater *domestic investment*, retraining and greater public spending.

(d) *Improving supply*: Control over *domestic inflation* and *higher productivity* will both make British goods more competitive. The monetarists would use monetary policy to achieve the former and trade union reform to influence the latter, thereby invigorating the supply side of the economy. Other initiatives such as privatization, the abolition of some wage councils, and reducing the real value of unemployment benefits have all indirectly made *labour markets more elastic*. The hope is that greater efficiency and lower unit costs will result so that British goods restore their competitiveness.

Britain has the second lowest percentage of GDP in fixed capital formation throughout OECD nations at 16 per cent (EEC average 19 per cent).

This policy, unlike the previous three, is more microeconomic and less generalized in its approach.

8.4.4 *Exchange rates*

Currently, exchange rates are *floating* – they fluctuate daily in accordance with changes in demand and supply. In theory the demand for sterling is a *derived demand* reflecting the demand for British exports, and the supply shows the demand for British imports. However, the growth of international financial speculation is such that capital flows of '*hot money*' are a more important determinant of a currency's value than trading activities.

In the nineteenth and early twentieth centuries, exchange rates were *fixed* in terms of gold. However, the lack of gold and the growth of world trade ended the *gold standard*, as other currencies, such as dollar and pound, became acceptable. From 1931 to 1947 the pound floated uneasily. In 1947 a system of fairly fixed exchange rates was established, in which a central bank had some *discretion* (1 per cent band either way) in their *management*. This system ended in 1971 because confidence in the main reserve currency, the dollar, fell and *speculative assaults* on overvalued currencies destabilized the foreign exchange markets.

The case for floating exchange rates:

(a) The rate *adjusts automatically* to a balance of payments disequilibrium. This gives a government freedom to pursue internal economic policies without a balance of payments constraint.

(b) *Less speculation* will occur because speculators could lose, whereas with fixed rates they had a one-way bet which could not lose.

(c) *More efficient resource allocation* because the exchange rates are sensitive to, and reflect, underlying economic conditions.

(d) *Large supply of currency reserves* is unnecessary, as balance of payments deficit leads to exchange rate depreciation and subsequent balance.

Criticisms of the floating system:

(a) There is *no automatic adjustment* e.g. persistent overvaluation of the pound in 1980–5 which accentuated deindustrialization. Economic freedom for a government can become irresponsible.

Britain finally left gold standard in 1931.

The central bank would buy/sell currency so that the exchange rate stayed within its limits.

The speculators usually won and never lost with fixed exchange rates. They sold currencies which they believed to be 'overvalued' and thereby gained if the currency was devalued. However, if it maintained its value, they could buy back the same amount of currency without loss.

In theory resources would be quickly reallocated into profitable enterprises around the world. Such international mobility of factors is very unrealistic, except perhaps for capital.

An index of real exchange rate values showed the pound persistently well over 100, varying from 150 to 115 between 1980–5.

(b) *Speculation has increased*, particularly at the margins. Exchange rates now tend to equalize the expected rates of return on capital rather than underlying inflation.

(c) *Currency fluctuations are destabilizing* and make trade more risky because an exchange rate appreciation will cut the profit margins on exports.

This problem of spot prices can be partly off-set by buying currency in advance in the 'forward market'.

(d) *Dirty floating* has been prevalent because some central banks intervene so that their government's exchange rate target is obtained.

There are three main theories which explain why exchange rates change:

Purchasing power parity (PPP)

Thus if Britain's inflation is 2 per cent below world averages, the pound will appreciate by 2 per cent.

Raising interest rates to keep the pound up has been more concerned with inflation control than domestic consumption.

The retail price index is inappropriate as it does not cover internationally traded goods and services exclusively. Unit wage costs might be a better deflator.

This theory suggests that exchange rates will settle at the point where their *international purchasing power* is equalized. Unfortunately, the empirical *evidence* does not show a constant 'real' exchange rate, with the pound generally overvalued. This probably reflects activities of *speculators*, with faith in a petro-currency, and relatively *high interest rates* to attract foreign capital. Also, there are technical problems with PPP such as the choice of *base year* and the measurement of *inflation*.

Keynesian view

Mainly because of the *distorting influences* above, they do not believe that the real exchange rate adjusts automatically. There is no equilibrium in short or medium term.

Monetarist approach

Quantity theory of money again.

This would be rational behaviour because the speculators expect an appreciation from the growth performance and monetary restraint.

The external price of a currency is just another price which is determined by *market forces*. Thus changes in exchange rates result from changes in *domestic money* supply. An increase in British money supply of 10 per cent when other nations hold their money supply constant will cause a 10 per cent depreciation. The lower exchange rate value then compensates for the higher production price resulting from domestic inflation induced by monetary growth. *Economic growth* will raise an exchange rate because it absorbs the monetary expansion and encourages international financiers to buy the currency.

Floating exchange rates have reduced the work and influence of the *International Monetary Fund* (IMF). The IMF began with the fixed exchange rate regime and was active in maintaining exchange rate stability. It *policed the system* and approved devaluations. This role ended in 1972. However, IMF continues to lend to member nations, via *special oil facilities* and *special drawing rights*, in order to increase world *liquidity*. Together with the *World Bank*, the IMF provides aid and advice to the developing world.

IMF stand by credit to British government 1976 required changes in government policy i.e. cuts in public expenditure.

8.4.5   *European monetary system*

Not Britain, who declined to join. However, there has been strong pressure recently (1987) for Britain to participate because of the stability it gives to exchange rates.

This is a *pegged* exchange rate system. It was launched in 1979 with the objective of creating a *zone of monetary stability*. The currencies of the participating members are *fixed* against one another, via the European currency unit (ecu), but allowed to *fluctuate* within a ±2¼ per cent band (Italy has ±6 per cent margin). Once a currency reaches its trigger point against another, both central banks must intervene. If their action fails to restore stability, a realignment is allowed.

The ecu is a basket of the participant currencies.

There have been only eleven realignments in eight years.

It is widely accepted that the EMS has *reduced* exchange rate *volatility* and increased the predictability of members' currencies. This stability promotes confidence and *reduces uncertainty* in trade. The deutschemark has provided a *solid anchor* for the system and been attractive to members because of its low inflation. However, the system does require *greater co-operation* in demand management policies between countries. It also necessitates an active *interest rate policy* to signal to financial markets a government's resolve to hold an exchange rate at a certain level.

British membership would be logical, given our *trade with Europe* and West Germany, in particular; and the close *informal co-operation* in the Group of Seven. In addition, it would give the financial markets greater *confidence* in the pound and make it less susceptible to overshooting. However, opponents of entry fear that co-operation with other countries would mean that Britain has to adopt policies which are inappropriate. This would limit the *economic sovereignty* of the government, as its policies would have to converge with others, notably the Germans and French.

This has led one commentator to suggest that Britain is in essence, a shadow member. Between February–July 1987 the pound fluctuated within 2 per cent of deutschemark.

Revision questions

1 (a) Identify the main objectives of government economic policy.
  (b) What is meant by 'indicative planning' and how can this be used to achieve these objectives?

(CIMA November 1986)

2 Outline the main causes of unemployment. How far can fiscal policy lower aggregate unemployment? (ICAI Autumn 1984)

Part Three
Examination Questions

Chapter 1

Question 1.1

How does the market mechanism work to solve the basic economic problem and co-ordinate the activities of the workforce?

First the student needs to identify the basic economic problem as being the lack of resources necessary to enable people to fulfil their wants. Society, consequently, must seek to maximize welfare with limited resources, making choices with regard to the allocation of resources. These choices largely revolve round what to produce, how to produce and for whom to produce. The market mechanism, which is also known as the price mechanism, is one of three methods of allocating resources.

The student must outline how the market mechanism operates in allocating resources, the interaction between consumer and supplier, the use of the money vote and how these combine to influence price and production levels and distribution.

The market mechanism places the consumer in direct contact with the supplier. The consumers then indicate a preference for a good by means of a money vote i.e. by the amount they are willing to pay for a particular good. The use of this money vote indicates to the supplier the consumers' preference. Although the amount of money vote varies between each individual consumer, the market mechanism takes the distribution of market spending power as given.

The supplier, within the market mechanism, will respond to consumers' money votes by supplying a number of different goods at different prices, each price being determined by production costs. As the market mechanism is allowed to work, however, an equilibrium price for both consumers and sellers will be reached, at which the amount supplied by the producer is at a price equal to the amount the purchaser is willing to pay. Thus, in a market mechanism consumers wanting more tea and less coffee would indicate that they were willing to see tea prices rise and as the demand for coffee falls so too will its price. This will result in changing production levels of tea and coffee.

Money votes therefore determine what is produced and who receives the goods. The relative prices of capital and labour determine how the goods are produced, and these prices are, in turn, determined by demand and supply.

Question 1.2

Economics has been described as the study of wealth. Discuss the adequacy of this definition, making clear the nature and scope of the subject.

The description of economics as the study of wealth suggests the central importance of price in the relationship between people and their environments, because prices are used to value resources and thus identify wealth. The price, or exchange value, of goods and services results from the scarcity of resources and competing ends for which those resources could be used. The person who has wealth has command over scarce resources, with wealth being determined by the value or utility placed on those resources.

The scarcity of resources and competing ends for their use create a basic economic problem. The scarcity results in the need for choices to be made. A choice represents a cost, the cost of alternatives which are forgone; the real cost of a resource is therefore the opportunity cost.

Various 'economic systems' operate in order to distribute the scarce resources. A market economy is an economic system in which resources are distributed on the basis of wealth i.e. those who can work and earn in order to pay for the scarce resources can get them. An alternative system is the command economy where all needs are determined and met by the planning and organization of a central planning agency. A third economic system, the mixed economy, is a combination of the other two.

Economics is not an exact science because it is not based on certainties, rather it is based on uncertainties and economic laws therefore can only be drawn up on the basis of 'other things being equal'. Thus economics is a social science as it concerns human behaviour and choice, investigating also the wide-ranging factors which affect those choices.

Chapter 2

Question 2.1

Economies of scale can provide major advantages in cost savings and consequently may lead to competitive pricing. Discuss.

First, the student must provide a definition or show an understanding of economies of scale as the reduction of the average cost per unit due to large-scale production which spreads fixed costs over more units.

The economies of scale may stem from internal or external sources. The student needs to identify the various categories and sources of the internal and external economies, explaining how they contribute to cost savings and competitive pricing.

Thus, the four main categories of internal economies are technical, managerial, trading and financial. Technical economies arise out of the use of advanced machinery and linking of processes which is facilitated by large-scale production. Technical economies contribute to cost savings in terms of time, transport and fuel consumption.

Managerial economies are gained from the opportunities for specialization resulting from large-scale production. This creates economy through the ability to delegate and by means of functional specialization.

Trading economies reducing costs are gained from large-scale production in terms of gaining significant discounts from bulk buying and making cost savings in distribution and advertising by means of bulk selling.

Cost savings are made through financial economies of scale, largely because the larger firm can more readily raise capital because there are greater sources of capital available to it, because of size and reputation; and because the cost of credit is lower for the larger firm.

As far as external economies are concerned the concentration of industry is one such economy, producing lower transport costs and allowing the development of mutual services such as financial services, transport services, and research services, all of which reduce the cost of use for the individual firm.

The student must then point to the fact that the reduction in marginal costs produced by the external and internal economies may allow the larger firm to accept a lower price per unit for the same goods as those produced by smaller firms – thus creating competitive pricing.

Question 2.2

In what ways may businesses integrate? Give reasons why they may wish to do so.

A business may integrate in a number of ways. Firms may combine into one organization as a merger in which shareholders agree to exchange old shares for shares in the new firm in agreed proportions. This merger takes place on equal terms although a merger may take the form of an absorption where one firm is stronger.

A takeover is a form of combination in which one party is unwilling for the combination to take place.

There are three main types of integration. Horizontal integration occurs when firms in the same industry, and at the same stage in production, combine. This type of merger occurs most frequently in retailing. If the merger is between suppliers or customers rather than competitors, this constitutes vertical integration. This integration may be backwards towards the source of supply, for example, Ross Foods, which sells frozen food, purchasing its own fleet of trawlers. It may be forwards towards the finished product; or it may be both.

A third type of integration is that of diversification when one firm expands into an industry with which it was previously unconnected.

The reasons for a firm integrating are many and varied. As far as horizontal integration is concerned the firm's motivation or purpose may be that of gaining economies of scale, or to gain an increase in market share, or to facilitate a pooling of technology. Vertical integration may be undertaken to eliminate transaction costs, or to create more entry barriers for prospective competitors or to secure supplies. Technical efficiency may be another reason, in providing for a physical proximity and continuity of processes. As with horizontal integration, economies of scale may be another reason for vertical integration.

The reasons for diversification are usually those of minimizing risks, making full use of expertise and economies of scale in administration.

Finally, in an absorption or takeover, the main reason may be the reorganization of the financial structure.

Chapter 3

Question 3.1

Define a monopoly. Explain how it may be contrary to public interest and how government policy protects the public interest.

The student must first define a monopoly. It is a market with one seller or supplier of a good where firms are not free to enter the market and where the single firm can influence the price of the market, because there is an absence of substitutes.

Explanation then needs to be made of *how* a monopoly is not in the best interests of the public. The fundamental reason which needs to be pointed out is that a monopoly creates a situation in which fewer goods are produced at a higher price. The student needs to explain how this arises; this is best done by means of the following diagram.

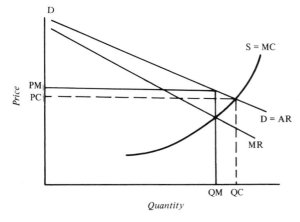

MC = S is supply curve

DD is industry demand

The diagram should be explained. The industry demand curve is also the demand curve of the monopolist, with equilibrium being achieved at MC = MR. The equilibrium of the monopolist is at price PM and quantity QM, where price exceeds marginal cost. Thus it can be seen that the monopolist produces less at a higher price than the perfectly competitive industry.

The student should now address the area of government policy towards monopolies and how it seeks to protect the public interest against monopolistic markets.

The primary focus of government policy is on control of monopolies through administrative investigation by the Monopolies and Mergers Commission. This body seeks to examine existing monopoly situations and those in which a monopoly may arise. If a monopoly is found to be against the public interest then the Secretary of State has powers to transfer property from one body to another, re-allocate stocks or shares or adjust contracts.

Another area of policy is nationalization. This policy creates monopolies in industries providing public utilities such as electricity and gas in order to protect public interest from their needs being placed second to profit motives.

Question 3.2

Define each of the following terms: price, income and cross elasticities of demand. Describe briefly the factors that determine each of them.

Price elasticity of demand, or demand elasticity, is a matter of responsiveness of demand to changes in price. Demand is elastic if a small change in price leads to a greater percentage change in demand. If the percentage change in demand is less, demand is inelastic. Demand elasticity is estimated by:

$$\frac{\text{Percentage change in quantity demanded}}{\text{Percentage change in price}}$$

If the demand is elastic a fall in price increases total expenditure on the good and a rise in price reduces it. When demand is inelastic a fall in price reduces total expenditure and a rise in price increases it. If the calculation of demand elasticity gives a figure greater than one, demand is elastic. If it is less than one, demand is inelastic.

Demand elasticity is determined by two factors, the availability of substitutes and the proportion of income spent on the good. The greater the number of substitutes available, the more elastic will be demand. When a small proportion of income is spent on a good such as salt a change in price is unlikely to have much effect on demand which will therefore be inelastic. Demand elasticity will vary over time for it may take some time for buyers to react to a price change and find substitutes.

Income elasticity of demand, or income elasticity, is concerned with the effect on demand of a change in income. Demand is income elastic if a change in income leads to a greater percentage change in demand. If the percentage change is smaller, demand is income inelastic. Income elasticity is estimated by:

$$\frac{\text{Percentage change in quantity demanded}}{\text{Percentage change in income}}$$

For most goods income elasticity will be positive and an increase in income will lead to an increase in their demand. Such goods are called normal goods. There are a few goods with negative income elasticity where demand falls as income rises. These are called inferior goods.

The income elasticity of goods depends on the stage of development of an economy in terms of income levels. In wealthy developed countries food and basic clothing have a low income elasticity. The demand for goods such as motor cars, washing machines and foreign holidays rises rapidly as incomes increase and the demand for these is highly income elastic. In very poor countries even basic commodities will have a high income elasticity. As incomes rise the consumption of these will level off and other goods will take their place.

Cross-elasticity of demand is concerned with the effects of a change in the price of one good on the demand for another good. There will be a high cross-elasticity of demand between goods which are good substitutes for each other, for example, between two brands of baked beans. Here a rise in the price of one brand will result in an increase in the demand for the other. A different situation arises when the two goods are complements and are consumed together, for example, coffee and sugar. Here a rise in the price of coffee may reduce the demand for coffee *and* for sugar. In both the above cases measurements of the cross-elasticity of demand relate the change in the price of one good to changes in the demand for the other.

Chapter 4

Question 4.1

To what extent is a trade union able to achieve and increase the real income of its members?

First we need to define real income and thus distinguish it from money or nominal income. Real income is measured in terms of spending power; thus money income may remain the same but if prices rise then real income has fallen.

The principal role of a trade union is to secure better wages and working conditions for its membership. Its success in this role will depend on a number of factors including size of the industry, size of membership, whether there is a closed shop etc. The most dominant factors however are the demand for the particular labour and the economic well-being of the particular industry. If demand for labour is high then the union will be able to demand more and gain more as the industry will put any increased labour costs onto prices. If the market for the industry is poor then employers will be reluctant to put costs onto selling price, in order to meet increased labour costs.

An industry has three alternatives in meeting increased labour costs. It can improve productivity by reducing unit cost and improving work practices. It can reduce its labour costs by reducing labour and increasing capital in its place. Often capital-intensive industries have high productivity and are able to pay high wages to their workforce. Key workers in such industries can press for wage increases quite effectively. A third alternative is to meet increased labour costs by increasing prices. This can lead to inflationary trends as an increase in prices will in turn prompt more wage demands.

It is evident that in a capital-intensive industry which is successful a strong union can increase the real income of its members both in the short run and, to some extent, in the long run. If the union presses for wage increases without improving productivity however the firm will often seek alternative technology.

It is the ability to exert monopoly pressure in inelastic market conditions which determines whether a union can increase real income for its members. Most often wage increases are nominal as inflation erodes any gains, whilst members of weaker trade unions are left behind.

Question 4.2

Describe and explain the measurement of national income and analyze whether it is a reliable measure of the standard of living.

First the student must provide some definition of what national income is i.e. the total of all factor incomes earned in the production of the national product.

The question is best approached by describing, in turn, the three ways in which national income can be measured. One approach to the measurement of national income is that of the level of output of goods and services within the economy. The value of this output is measured in monetary terms in order to allow the summation of items with quite different characteristics.

A second approach is that of expenditure. This approach to measuring economic activity is based on the fact that payment for output generates factor incomes. The student needs to explain what expenditure is and how it is calculated and therefore should list the five classes of expenditure recognized in the national accounts as follows:

(a)   Consumers' expenditure.
(b)   Current expenditure on goods and services by public authorities.
(c)   Gross domestic fixed capital formation.

(d)   The value of the physical increase in stocks and work-in-progress.

(e)   Exports and property income from abroad.

The third approach to the measurement of national income is the income method, which adds together all the different categories of factor incomes. The student needs to explain the term 'factor income'; that it is used to avoid the possibility of double counting certain incomes in the form of transfer payments.

The student needs to indicate that national income is the most reliable measurement of the standard of living but needs also to acknowledge its failings. The most significant failings of national income lie in its ignoring of non-monetary transactions, whilst its use of money as the measure results in the possibility of inflation eroding the real value of the figures.

The question asks whether national income is a reliable measure of the *standard of living*; the student, therefore, needs to explain what is meant by the term 'standard of living' in order to provide a full answer to the question.

Standard of living does not measure the 'quality of life'. Factors which contribute to the quality of living such as the availability of social amenities, increase in leisure time etc. are not measured by national income. Indeed if such factors are achieved they may reduce productive potential or employment which will be reckoned by the national income measure as a reduction in the standard of living. It is evident, therefore, that the standard of living and quality of life are not synonymous.

Chapter 5

Question 5.1

'A commercial banker's role is to convert illiquid assets into usable credit.'

(a)   Explain this statement and state why this role is important.

(b)   What limits a banker's ability to create credit?

(CIMA May 1986)

In the first part of the question, a student needs to *define* the main terms in the statement. This means explaining that a commercial bank has *share-holders*, who seek *profits* from the bank's function as a *retailer* of money. *Assets* should be distinguished from liabilities, with suitable examples being given.

Liquid (e.g. cash) and illiquid assets (e.g. advances) need to be identified. The way in which *credit* is created should be outlined. Then the relationship between assets and credit can be explained, with reference to *cash* (and other) *ratios*, *prudential behaviour* and *profit maximization*. However, it must be pointed out that *not* all illiquid assets are converted into usable credit.

There are many *constraints* on credit creation, and each should be examined in turn. For instance, the *behaviour of other banks* is crucial. If one bank expands credit much faster than other banks, it will continually suffer indebtedness at clearing and run down its balance at the Bank of

England which is treated as part of its cash base. Eventually the bank will not be able to repay depositors and public confidence will be undermined. Also, other *financial intermediaries* may attract depositors, by higher interest rates, and thereby activate funds removal from the banks.

However, the most significant limitations are the banks themselves and the Bank of England. A bank may *raise its cash ratio* and thus have less credit-creating potential. The *Bank of England* may *sell bills* and/or bonds or *raise interest rates* in order to lower the demand for any credit, which a commercial bank is willing to offer.

Question 5.2

(a)   How may a government seek to control the supply of money? (12)
(b)   How effective are the methods of control likely to be? (8)

(CACA June 1986)

The supply of money has become a central economic issue with the emergence of the *monetarists*. They seek to control it in order to restrict inflation. A student should quickly mention the difficulties of *measuring money* and *Goodhart's Law* which states that once a target measure of money is chosen for control it immediately becomes distorted, as the banking sector seek to circumvent it.

The two parts of the question are difficult to keep separate but in part (a) the methods at the government's disposal should be *described* whereas in part (b) they should be *analyzed* and discussed. Thus in part (a) the link between money supply and *PSBR* needs outlining in some detail. Also, the various weapons of *monetary policy*, which enable the Bank of England to exert influence over the commercial banks, should be applied.

The issue of effectiveness enables a student to criticize monetarist theory and cite recent evidence. The government's consistent *failure* to achieve money supply targets would suggest that its control is less than effective. Keynesians would explain this by reference to the *demand for money*, which in their view is the determinant of the supply of money. It could also be noted that there are *broad* and *narrow* measures of money supply and that government control of the former is less because of the nature of financial intermediaries involved.

As a conclusion it might be suggested that 'influence' is a better description than 'control'. Furthermore, in a democracy which has a capitalist banking sector, excessive government interference might undermine the confidence and ability of commercial banks to achieve profits.

Chapter 6

Question 6.1

'If a production tax is imposed on a commodity, the effect on producers, consumers and the market will depend on the relative elasticities of demand and supply.' Explain.

(CIMA May 1987)

You need to define the terms in the quotation. A production tax is an *indirect tax*, such as VAT, which raises the sale price. It thus affects the *conditions of supply* and causes a *shift* of the supply curve to the left. You should draw a simple diagram to illustrate the effects of this in terms of higher prices and lower quantity demanded.

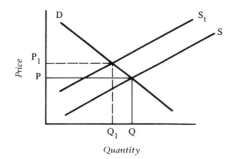

The concept of *elasticity* should be described, with the different types clearly distinguished. Several variations need to be applied to the question, showing that the proportionate change in quantity demanded will be less but the increase in price will be more, the greater the *inelasticity of demand*. Somewhat differently the greater the *inelasticity of supply* the higher the price rise and the greater the fall in quantity demanded.

The third stage is to consider the effect of quantity and price changes on the consumer and the producer. This brings in the real *incidence* of the tax. A diagram can be used to illustrate the burden borne by the producer and the consumer respectively.

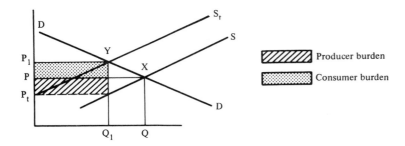

In this case the producer suffers more than the consumer but the overall consumer surplus is lowered from PXD to P_1YD. The market for the commodity contracts to Q_1 because of the higher price P_1. Another diagram with a different set of elasticities is needed for contrast.

In conclusion, it could be pointed out that these burdens may change in the long run, depending on producers' behaviour and structure of market.

Question 6.2

Outline the main causes of unemployment. How far can fiscal policy lower aggregate unemployment?

(ICAI Autumn 1984)

This question has a fairly straightforward first part. The many suggested causes of unemployment should be mentioned with stress placed on the main categories i.e. *structural, demand deficiency, frictional, technological.* Also, the general theory relating *inflation* and unemployment via *money wages* should be outlined, with passing reference to the Phillips curves.

The second part is really an appraisal of the *Keynesian approach* to demand management with unemployment reduction as the primary policy objective. As such you need to define *fiscal policy* and show how tax and public spending changes can be used to change output and therefore employment. The underlying *assumptions* of the theory need explaining and then questioning. The 'how far' in the title leads you on to a discussion of the *effectiveness* of such a policy, and its *side-effects* (e.g. inflation). You should also bring in the *monetarist criticisms* of this policy which characterized 1960s and 1970s economic management in Britain.

The monetarist alternative might be briefly introduced as part of a balanced conclusion. In your summary you could also mention policies, other than fiscal policy, which might have an impact on unemployment e.g. *monetary* and *incomes* policies.

Chapter 7

Question 7.1

(a)   *Define and explain the marginal and average propensities to save.   (6)*
(b)   *Demonstrate the consequences of an increase in the flow of savings in an economy.*
(14)
(ACA June 1984)

Part (a) involves straightforward recall of the Keynesian theory. The average propensity to save is the proportion of *disposable income* which is saved. This is calculated by saving/income (give an actual example). APS is *negative* at low income levels but *positive* at high income levels.

The MPS shows the change in saving with changes in income. For instance, if an increase in income of £20 produces an increase in saving of £2 then the MPS = 0.1 (2/20). The MPS also rises with income levels.

In part (b) of the question, the concepts of MPS + APS need applying to the economy. The *Keynesian model* provides a good starting point. Higher savings mean *more leakages* from the circular flow and therefore less potential for growth. Assuming unchanged income then lower consumption occurs with the usual effects on demand, output and employment. This could be shown on the Keynesian cross-diagram. The motives behind the increased savings should also be outlined; i.e. changes in interest rates and inflation.

However, in the *long run* more savings could be beneficial to an economy. If they are translated into *investment*, via the financial institutions, then the productive capacity of the economy will be enhanced and economic growth activated.

Question 7.2

(a)   *Explain what is meant by equilibrium when referring to the general*
      level of output and employment.   *(10)*
(b)   *What will be the effect on output and employment of each of the*
      following changes?
         (i) An *increase in investment (5)*
         (ii) An *increase in imports (5)*

(CACA June 1985)

The concept of equilibrium is central to much of macroeconomics. It is a state of rest when *planned expenditure* equals *planned output* and national income is in balance. Equilibrium does *not* mean full utilization of all resources. In practice all economies are in disequilibrium because planned and realized activities do not coincide. *Inelasticity* makes micromarkets unbalanced and thus prevents overall equilibrium.

The simple *Keynesian model* shows that when aggregate demand equals aggregate supply the economy is in equilibrium.

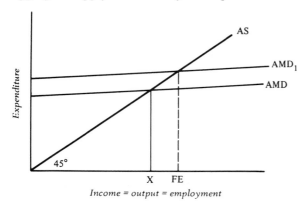

Income = output = employment

However, at output X there is not necessarily full employment. This could be achieved by shifting AMD upwards (Keynesian demand management policies) so that equilibrium is achieved with the full use of labour resources.

In part (b), (i) again a diagram will be most useful. An *injection* such as an increase in investment, *ceteris paribus*, raises AMD and thus induces higher employment via the *multiplier* effect. It enhances the productive capacity of the economy and thereby raises growth potential. Thus in the *long run*, assuming the investment is efficient output will be raised. A distinction could be made between *capital deepening* (machines replacing labour) and *capital widening*.

An increase in imports will affect equilibrium levels of output and employment. Assuming that the imports supplant domestic goods, rather than filling a growing market which home firms at 100 per cent capacity cannot accommodate, the effect will be destabilizing. Some domestic output will remain unsold, *stocks* will accumulate and the aspirations of suppliers will be thwarted. Thus in the next period they will produce less and shed labour. The effects will be compounded because the import represents a *leakage* from the circular flow and so aggregate demand will be lower, reducing national income and causing a backward multiplier effect.

Chapter 8

Question 8.1

(a)   *Why are changes in the price of oil significant in international trade?*
                                                                       (6)

(b)   *Outline the possible consequences of:*
      (i) An *increase*
      (ii) A *fall in the price of oil*   *(14)*
                                                        (CIMA November 1986)

Oil is an *essential* commodity for production because it has *no real substitute*. Thus price changes, such as the 1973 quadrupling, have dramatic effects on individual economies. For instance Japan as a large importer would face a large *debit* on its balance of payments. Generally, changes affect the *volume* of world trade. A fall in price will tend to stimulate world trade, while a rise will lead to recession because the capacity of nations to buy other imports is reduced. Also, the growth of international financial speculation has meant that countries with indigenous oil resources find their *exchange rates appreciating* when oil prices rise. This tends to destabilize the world economy.

In part (b) more specific effects need considering. An increase in oil prices benefits oil exporters whose *balance of payments* and *national incomes* gain. The income could be used to generate *growth* or for investment abroad. In the 1970s the latter disrupted international money markets, seeking high interest rates and destabilizing exchange rates.

In contrast oil importers suffer *rising production costs* and possibly recession. When this happened in the 1970s the developing nations were afflicted by not only dearer oil but *smaller markets* for their exports in the recession-ridden advanced economies. However, in the long term such increases stimulate the development of *alternatives*, more *efficient use* of existing resources and greater conservation.

The consequences of an oil price fall are not necessarily all good. Oil exporters suffer *lower incomes* and a reduced capacity to trade, although oil importers have their balance of payments and cost burdens alleviated. However, oil resources may be used up more quickly and squandered.

Question 8.2

(a) What factors determine exchange rates?   *(12)*
(b) How do you account for the high price of the US dollar in relation to other currencies in 1984 and 1985?   *(8)*

(CACA June 1986)

In part (a) you need to quickly distinguish between the differing exchange rate systems – *fixed*, *managed* and *floating*. You should concentrate on the latter which is operative nowadays. Foreign exchange is demanded for *trade* and *speculation*, with demand for the latter at least ten times greater. An exchange rate will appreciate if speculators' demand for it increases because of attractive interest rates, faith in a government's economic policies, relative inflation and petrocurrency considerations. Each should be explained separately.

The textbook theory is that a currency is sought in order to pay for that country's exports. Thus, successful exporting will produce a balance of payments surplus and an appreciating exchange rate, assuming no speculative effects.

The second part of the question is dated now, but it shows the importance of contemporary knowledge and the regular reading of the financial columns.

The dollar's strength in this period was the result of high interest rates, America's strong domestic performance, falling oil prices (with the break-up of OPEC) and the European recession.

Part Four
Examination Technique

Common pitfalls

It is surprising that candidates do not take sufficient care in presentation. Examiners can only mark what they can read and should not be expected to spend more time on untidy and illegible scripts than on those well presented. This is perhaps reflected in the fact that a significant number of candidates approach examinations in economics ill-prepared in terms of knowledge of economics and examination technique. The candidate who is prepared can gain considerable confidence from the fact that he is pitting his wits against others who have failed before even entering the examination room.

'If only candidates would actually set out to answer the question set' – one wonders how many times this has to be said but the problem still exists. Many candidates write everything they know about a topic rather than answering the specific question. This results in many answers that are long, repetitive and contain much irrelevant material; it is not enough to regurgitate pages of a textbook which have the same key words. Far too many candidates fail to read the question, frequently focusing simply upon a key phrase or 'buzz word'. While it is beneficial to gain examination practice and an insight into structuring answers to particular questions it is *not* advisable to memorize entire answers to questions in the hope that they will be repeated. The examiner is charged with the specific responsibility of producing unique questions. While the same topic may be examined regularly the same question will not be asked. Having spent effort learning answers by heart there is a tendency to produce these irrespective of the emphasis of the specific question on the current paper.

These are not the only causes of irrelevant answers; insufficient knowledge of the subject area means candidates are unable to identify the concepts relevant to the question. There is a tendency therefore to clutch at straws.

Candidates must learn the importance of producing clear, well-structured answers, applying concepts and theories to the requirements of the question. Working through this book gives students experience of doing exactly that process, linking the key theories and concepts of the syllabus to the requirements of examination questions. The process of analysis frequently rests on a well-presented comparison of advantages and disadvantages, costs and benefits etc.

Papers are set on the basis that a proper allocation of writing time allows the candidates to meet the requirements of the question adequately. Appropriate time allocation through structured answers is crucial. Clarity of expression, logic of argument and concise lucid English are all important requirements for examination purposes and allow the candidate to answer the question in the time set. Incorrect allocation of time often means that candidates who are capable of passing the examination will fail. It is a reality of examinations that it is much more difficult to gain the last quarter of available marks for a question than it is to gain the first ten marks on a twenty-mark question. It is therefore extremely foolhardy to write at length on one answer with a consequent inability to complete all the questions required.

Specific problems

Economics frequently requires the drawing of diagrams to illustrate a conceptual relationship between two variables. Indeed even if not explicitly required by the question many answers would be dramatically improved by the inclusion of a diagram. However it is important to realize that diagrams demonstrate lack of understanding as forcefully as understanding. There seems to be partial recognition of this by students in that when candidates are unsure of an appropriate response there will be a tendency to obscure diagrams or omit labels for axes. In order to gain marks for a diagram candidates must ensure that there is a title, axes are labelled and any curves etc. on the illustration are clearly marked. An examiner commenting on an examination in 1986 highlights this point. 'Many candidates displayed a very uncertain grasp of basic principles, having relied on rote learning without understanding. This was shown in particular through wrong labelling of diagrams. . . . For example, it was only too common for candidates to label the AC (average cost) curve as MR (marginal revenue) and show the point of intersection with the marginal cost (MC) curve as MC = MR. Another common error was to transpose AC/MC and AR/MR, in both cases showing that while the diagrammatic representation itself was accurate, the relationship between the curves was not understood.' This reinforces the need to think about and understand basic relationships.

Examiners' comments

A study of examiners' reports for a range of accountancy bodies of a period of time reinforces many of the points made earlier. It also highlights two key features. First it is important that candidates have a clear grasp of fundamental concepts. These would include opportunity costs, basic demand and supply theory in all its aspects and applications and equilibrium analysis. It is interesting that examiners often highlight that supply, in particular, is not well understood. This clear grasp of fundamental concepts must then be applied to the precise situation referred to in the question. The inclusion of irrelevant, often accurate, information distracts the student from the purpose of answering the original question.

Second, candidates need to study the paper as a whole before answering particular questions. There is a tendency for candidates to duplicate answers on papers where examiners explore issues such as distribution of resources, and location of industry on the same paper. Clearly these topics are not the same and unless candidates explore issues in the context of the whole paper this mistake becomes possible. A moment of reflection should show that examiners are not going to ask for exactly the same application in two answers.

Exam technique

Remain calm! Remember you are better prepared than many other exam entrants. Calmness allows more logical thought and this is important.

A choice (within an examination) can be a painful decision. However it is a positive opportunity for candidates to select those questions that they can answer most appropriately. It is therefore essential to spend a few minutes reading the whole paper to identify the requirements of the questions and see which are most readily fulfilled on the basis of your understanding and knowledge.

The questions selected should then be considered in more detail. Read the question carefully, thinking about the exact requirements you must fulfil to answer it. Structure an answer including all the key points you think necessary. Remember that questions requesting discussion etc. are often logical comparison rather than open-ended verbage.

The structure to your answer allows the presentation of a logical, concise answer which is not distracted by irrelevancies *but* does not forget key points because they have been noted. The question itself may be broken down into sections which aids the structure of your answer and remember to weight material according to marks available. Note that frequently candidates make the mistake of spending twice as long on a two-part question than on a single requirement – the marks are exactly the same and candidates must complete their coverage within the time available.

At the end of the examination check through your answers, in particular that diagrams are labelled correctly etc. Use all of the time available to you to best advantage.

Part Five
Test Paper

Time allowed: 3 hours
1 Attempt *five* questions only.
2 Answer the questions using:
   ● Effective arrangement and presentation
   ● Clarity of explanation
   ● Logical argument
   ● Clear diagrams where appropriate
   ● Clear and concise English
3 All questions carry equal marks.

1 How do free market and planned economies attempt to solve the basic economic problem? (20)

2 Briefly explain, with the aid of diagrams, when it becomes uneconomic for a competitive firm to remain in business. (10)

   Discuss whether a nationalized industry should be governed by the same criteria. (10)

3 What is the marginal productivity theory of wages. (12)

   Discuss its relevance to a modern economy. (8)

4 Explain the economic factors determining the location and size of a factory. (12)

   Show how the factors differ for a factory producing cars compared with one processing peas. (8)

5 Using economic analysis, discuss the relative merits and direct merits of indirect and direct taxes. (20)

6 Identify the main objectives of government economic policy. (8)

   Is inflation still a major problem in the United Kingdom? (12)

7 What is the supply of money? (5)

   How and why do governments attempt to control it? (15)

8 What factors determine exchange rates? (12)

   How do you account for the high price of £ sterling in 1987–8? (8)

Index